G000231343

Millwall Football Club
Official Yearbook 2004-05

Editorial
Deano Standing, Lucy Pepper, Johanne Springett & Marc Fiszman

Design
Daniel Anim-Kwapong, Ian Bull & Nick Thornton

Photography
Action Images, Brian Tonks

Copyright©Millwall Football Club 2004

Officials and Club Directory

Chairman: **Theo Paphitis**

Life President/Director: **Reg Burr**

Directors: **David Sullivan, Doug Woodward, Peter Mead, Ken Brown**

Club Address: **The Den, Millwall FC, Zampa Road, Bermondsey, SE16 3LN**

Main Number: **0207 232 1222**

Fax Number: **0207 231 9999**

Chief Executive: **Ken Brown**

General Manager: **Rick Bradbrook**

Club Secretary: **Yvonne Haines**

Marketing Manager: **Mark Cole**

Sales: **Pru Buckley**

Ticket Office Manager: **Graham Smith**

Stadium Manager: **Colin Sayer**

Operations & Security Advisor: **Ken Chapman**

Media: **Deano Standing, Lucy Pepper, Andrea Tennant**

Programme: **Paul Morrissey, Jacqui Fournier**

Community Scheme Manager: **Loo Brackpool**

Community Scheme: **Steve Baker, Lou Waller, Dicklan Selman, Yanike Thomas, Alex Eagle, Richard White, Tate Davidson, Vince Lee, Peter Dacres**

Lottery Manager: **Billy Neil**

Club Chaplin: **Owen Beament MBE**

Away Travel Office: **0207 740 0502**

Catering Department: **0207 740 0504**

ClubCall: **09068 400 300**

(calls charged at 60p per minute at all times)

Club Shop: **0207 231 9845**

Community Office: **0207 740 0503**

Enquiries: **0207 232 1222**

Enquiries Email: **info@millwallplc.com**

Credit Card Bookings: **0870 403 3357**

Home games only (24 hours a day, seven days a week, subject to booking fee) Calls charged at national rate.

Lottery Office: **0207 740 0502**

Matchday Hospitality: **0207 740 0501**

Sales and Promotions: **0207 740 0501**

TeamCard Helpline: **0207 740 0507**

Ticket Office: **0207 231 9999**

Ticket Office Email: **tickets@millwallplc.com**

Contents

From The Top

There is never a dull moment at The Den, but even by our own standards 2003/4 was a dramatic season for us.

Our aim last August was promotion to the Premiership, and in spite of a disappointing finish to the previous campaign, we believed that with our long-term injuries healed, we had a squad capable of achieving our goal.

By the middle of October it was clear that things were not quite right, and we took the painful decision to part company with Mark McGhee, a manager who in three years had taken Millwall from the Second Division to a position of strength in Division One.

It was a gamble, and initially the appointment of Dennis Wise and Ray Wilkins was designed to buy us a bit of time to find the right successor to Mark. As it turned out, Dennis and Ray quickly proved that they were the management team we needed and from Christmas onwards the team began to live up to its potential.

The season will ultimately be remembered by everyone for the FA Cup run, culminating in the first ever Final appearance in the club's history. It was certainly my dream to face Manchester United in an FA Cup Final, and the weekend in Cardiff along with the Semi-Final at Old Trafford will never be forgotten by any of us I'm sure.

What was disappointing, however, was that having got ourselves into a strong position to reach the Play-Offs, we slipped out of the top six in the last few games. Our priority remains the Premiership, and we will be redoubling our efforts towards reaching the top flight in 2004/5. We also have European football to look forward to, so it promises to be another very exciting year.

What pleased me as much as anything over the past 12 months has been the way in which Millwall Football Club and our fans have at last begun to receive some positive media coverage. This has been achieved thanks to a lot of hard work, not least by our supporters who were absolutely magnificent throughout the season and in Cardiff in particular. We have made great strides both on and off the field, and the adventure starts again on 7th August.

Theo Paphitis

Wisey's Word

The thing about football is that you cannot afford to look back. Last season is over and done with, we had some very enjoyable moments, particularly in the FA Cup, but that's all behind us now. The main thing I hope the players took away from the Cup Final was the desire to be playing the likes of Manchester United every week, because that has to be our focus this coming season.

It was a steep learning curve for me as a manager over the past few months. One thing which became very clear is that we need a stronger squad if we are to have a realistic chance of winning promotion.

Towards the end of last season we had too many of our senior players missing at various times, and whilst the youngsters came in and gave it their best shot, it demonstrated that we need more experience in the squad.

Our priority, therefore, has to be to bring in five or six new faces to give us plenty of cover all over the park. With the UEFA Cup also coming up this year, we're going to be playing 55 or 60 matches possibly and I'm determined that we will be better equipped to deal with that sort of schedule.

Ray and I are very much looking forward to the challenge in front of us, and hopefully the fans are as well.

We received magnificent support in the FA Cup last season, and we really want to see as many of you as possible down at The Den on a regular basis next season.

The passion and atmosphere that a big Millwall crowd can create makes such a difference to the players, and we're going to need that kind of backing week-in week-out over the coming months.

Dennis Wise

MILLWALL   2

WIGAN ATHLETIC   0

Form coming into fixture

MILLWALL	WIGAN ATH
N/A	N/A

🏃 Whelan	Jarrett 🧤
Hearn	Breckin
Gueret	Mitchell
Craig	Walsh
Sweeney	Kennedy

Goals from Dennis Wise and Tim Cahill got Millwall's campaign off to a flying start at the expense of Wigan.

The performance of Mark McGhee's Lions was a fitting tribute to popular coach Ray Harford, who had passed away in the early hours of the morning following a long battle with cancer.

Wise got the opener on 52 minutes, lashing the ball home from six yards after keeper John Filan had parried a Neil Harris penalty.

Inspirational skipper Wise then turned goal provider after 76 minutes, curling a pinpoint corner that Cahill met with a trademark header to give Filan no chance.

Following last season's opening day debacle at the hands of Rotherham United, this was the perfect way to erase that nightmare in front of a 10,898 Den crowd.

Millwall quickly adapted to the sweltering conditions, and there were just three minutes on the clock when the first scoring opportunity was created.

Paul Ifill latched onto Matt Lawrence's forward ball as he caught the Wigan defence napping, then flicked the ball beyond Filan's reach and sent a sizzling volley just wide of the mark.

The energetic Ifill went close again on 10 minutes, whilst Tony Warner produced a breathtaking fingertip save to somehow keep out Matt Jackson's point-blank header from a Nicky Eaden free kick.

But it was Millwall who continued to look the more likely to

Tim Cahill celebrates his goal.

Statistics

Season	Fixture		Fixture	Season
4	4	Shots On Target	9	9
6	6	Shots Off Target	3	3
0	0	Hit Woodwork	1	1
5	5	Caught Offside	5	5
4	4	Corners	6	6
17	17	Fouls	20	20

Juan jumps with John Filan.

Event Line			
15			Nethercott (Foul)
19			Dinning (Foul)
20			Eaden (Foul)
HALF-TIME 0-0			
53		⊙	Wise (Penalty Rebound)
55			Teale (Off) Jarrett (On)
58			McMillan (Foul)
61			De Vos (Off) Breckin (On)
62			Filan (Dissent)
71			Dinning (Off) Mitchell (On)
73			Juan (Off) Whelan (On)
73			Jarrett (Foul)
74		⊙	Cahill (Corner)
83			Ifill (Off) Hearn (On)
FULL-TIME 2-0			

League Table	P	W	D	L	F	A	Pts
1 Walsall	1	1	0	0	4	1	3
2 Stoke City	1	0	0	0	3	0	3
3 Wimbledon	1	1	0	0	3	1	3
4 Millwall	1	1	0	0	2	0	3
5 Nottm Forest	1	1	0	0	2	0	3

score. Cahill clipped the bar with a hooked shot after keeper Filan had fumbled a Wise corner, Juan mis-hit his shot agonisingly wide from just four yards, and Filan acrobatically tipped Ifill's effort clear.

Harris had a great chance to fire the home side ahead seconds before the break as he picked up a neat pass from Ifill in space; but instead of taking a touch to control the ball, Chopper went for a spectacular finish and lashed his first-time shot wide.

It proved to be a frustrating afternoon for last season's joint top scorer, particularly in the 52nd minute, when he stepped up to take a penalty awarded after Ifill had been hacked down by Jason De Vos.

Although Harris hit the ball well, not for the first time Filan flung himself across goal to avert the danger. On this occasion, however, the Wigan keeper could do nothing to prevent Wise beating him to the rebound and hammering home Millwall's first goal of the game.

Paul Jewell's side were clearly rattled at the spot-kick decision, and subsequently picked up two further bookings in quick succession to add to the three already recorded in referee Andy Hall's book.

Noel Whelan made his debut 18 minutes from time when he came on to replace fellow new-signing Juan, and within two minutes Millwall were further ahead courtesy of Cahill's header.

❝ Mark McGhee

The weather clearly didn't prove too hot for us because we won 2-0, but I thought both teams coped with it well, and showed an enormous amount of endeavour. ❞

❝ Theo Paphitis

We were all devastated by the news of Ray Harford's death even though we knew he was very ill. I'm only grateful we had the opportunity to assure him how much we valued, loved and appreciated him at Millwall. He was a fine coach and a lovely man. We will miss him greatly. ❞

MILLWALL 0

OXFORD UNITED 1

Warner

Lawrence Nethercott Ward Craig

Cahill Roberts Hearn Juan

Whelan Harris

Basham

Brown Townsley

Wanless Whitehead Ashton

Robinson Bound Crosby McNiven

Woodman

Gueret	Lovegrove
Dunne	Hackett
Phillips	Oldfield
Ryan	Omoyinmi
Braniff	Rawle

Mark Phillips takes control.

Statistics

8	Shots On Target	3
10	Shots Off Target	1
1	Hit Woodwork	0
2	Caught Offside	1
6	Corners	2
8	Fouls	13

Oxford striker Steve Basham bagged a 59th-minute winner to send shell-shocked Millwall crashing out of the Carling Cup at The Den.

Basham capitalised on some sloppy defending and let fly with a low drive that keeper Tony Warner got a hand to, only for the ball to loop over his head and into the back of the net.

It really was that sort of a night for a Lions side missing the energy and inspiration of injured duo Paul Ifill and Dennis Wise.

Ian Atkins' Third Division outfit had a simple game plan – defend in numbers, pack the midfield and try to cause problems on the counter-attack – and it worked a treat.

While Mark McGhee's men had their work cut out from the off against a compact, well-organised Oxford side, they might have made more of several gilt-edged scoring chances.

Juan and Neil Harris had already tested Andy Woodman in the visiting goal when Andy Roberts went agonisingly close to opening Millwall's account, when his 22nd-minute drive rattled the woodwork, with Woodman stranded.

Juan and Harris then combined to carve an opening for Charley Hearn, but he snatched at his shot and dragged the ball wide.

Millwall were denied what looked a certain penalty after 34

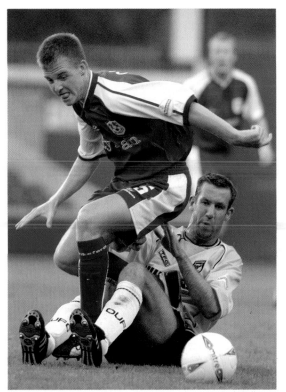
Tony Craig rides an Oxford challenge.

minutes when Jon Ashton grappled Harris to the ground, but referee Grant Hegley waved play on, much to the astonishment of the home fans and players alike.

The second half quickly settled into the same pattern as the first, with Millwall desperately trying to prise an opening and Oxford defending superbly as a unit.

Roberts tried his luck three minutes after the restart, but saw his angled drive flash wide of the post, as did Harris' shot from the edge of the area after 50 minutes.

The game was effectively settled in a five-minute spell during which the Lions should have scored, but Oxford did.

Sub Kevin Braniff saw keeper Woodman parry his angled drive on 54 minutes and the ball fell invitingly for Juan, but the little Brazilian somehow scooped the ball over the bar from barely four yards with the goal at his mercy.

The scale of that miss was evident within five minutes, as Oxford edged ahead through Basham.

The Lions' attempts to claw themselves back into the game became increasingly desperate, and Woodman was equal to efforts from Tim Cahill and Harris which had threatened to take the tie into extra time.

❝ Mark McGhee

We have put out our strongest available team, but it has not been enough. I thought they thoroughly deserved their win. A Cup run would have been nice. But you have to take the hand you are dealt. We have not got anything like the team at the moment which we will have eventually.

❞

Fixture Type: **Division One**

Date: **Sat, 16th August 2003**

Venue: **Stadium of Light**

Attendance: **24,877**

Referee: **A.R.Leake**

SUNDERLAND   0

MILLWALL   1

Form coming into fixture

SUNDERLAND	MILLWALL
L	W

```
                    Poom
Wright     Clark     Breen   McCartney
Piper   Thornton  Thirlwell  Kilbane
            Kyle   Proctor
          Harris   Whelan
Cahill    Hearn   Roberts    Wise
Ryan     Ward  Nethercott  Lawrence
              Warner
```

Gray
Oster
Stewart
Ingham
Whitley

Craig
Gueret
Dunne
Juan
Braniff

Statistics

Season	Fixture		Fixture	Season
19	9	Shots On Target	4	8
6	1	Shots Off Target	2	8
1	0	Hit Woodwork	0	0
2	0	Caught Offside	1	6
14	8	Corners	5	9
32	15	Fouls	20	37

Noel Whelan bagged an early winner to condemn sorry Sunderland to their 17th successive League defeat, and maintain Millwall's winning start to the First Division campaign.

Millwall edged ahead with barely five minutes on the clock when keeper Mart Poom could only parry Charley Hearn's shot, setting up an almighty goalmouth scramble, with Whelan eventually bundling the ball home from four yards.

The Lions, backed by some superb vociferous support from the fans throughout, created the best of the first-half chances against a Sunderland outfit clearly lacking in confidence and cohesion, and devoid of any real attacking ideas.

Neil Harris saw his eighth-minute cross held at the second attempt by the nervy Poom and Tim Cahill fired wide from 18 yards, before he and Whelan were denied by some desperate Sunderland defending.

Tony Warner had little to do during the opening half, but when he was called into action on 16 minutes, he comfortably held Sean Thornton's curling free kick.

Kevin Kilbane tried his luck from another free-kick, but was closer to hitting the roof of the stand than the back of the net, such was the inaccuracy of his woeful effort.

Stuart Nethercott celebrates victory.

Noel Whelan stabs home the winner.

At least the home side played with a bit more fire in their bellies after the break, forcing three corners in as many minutes, though The Lions dealt with them comfortably.

Warner was at his best to keep out Michael Proctor's stinging shot after 51 minutes, followed by a superlative save from Thornton.

The bleach-blond midfielder may have come in for some wolf-whistling from Millwall fans every time he had the ball, but he was the only Sunderland player who looked capable of breaching a resilient Lions rearguard and getting Mick McCarthy's men back in the game.

And the stocky playmaker nearly did just that in the 59th minute, only to be brilliantly denied by Warner once more. Andy Roberts was penalised for a foul on Kilbane around 22 yards out and Thornton took the free-kick, but Warner fingertipped his sweetly struck shot away at full stretch.

It was desperate stuff for Sunderland, and even after McCarthy made a triple substitution midway through the second half, The Lions were rarely troubled.

As much as the Black Cats huffed and puffed, Millwall defended superbly as a unit to deny their opponents.

In fact, the visitors might have added to their tally, with Dennis Wise forcing a smart stop from Poom and Whelan's half-volley flashing wide from distance.

Event Line		
5	⚽	Whelan (Open Play)
41	🟨	Cahill (Dissent)
HALF-TIME 0-1		
64	🟨	Thornton (Foul)
65	🟨	Roberts (Foul)
67	⇄	Kilbane (Off) Gray (On)
67	⇄	Piper (Off) Oster (On)
68	⇄	Proctor (Off) Stewart (On)
72	⇄	Hearn (Off) Craig (On)
FULL-TIME 0-1		

League Table	P	W	D	L	F	A	Pts
1 Stoke City	2	2	0	0	5	1	6
2 **Millwall**	2	2	0	0	3	0	6
3 C Palace	2	2	0	0	4	2	6
4 Reading	2	2	0	0	4	1	4
5 Walsall	2	1	1	0	4	1	4

Fixture Type: **Division One**

Date: **Sat, 23rd August 2003**

Venue: **The Den**

Attendance: **9,504**

Referee: **S.G.Tomlin**

MILLWALL 1

CREWE ALEXANDRA 1

A last-minute equaliser from Noel Whelan maintained Millwall's unbeaten record in the League, but it was a less-than-convincing performance by Mark McGhee's men.

Big Bob Peeters made his debut up front and showed some nice touches, but The Lions lacked the wit and invention to trouble a well-organised Crewe defence, with Clayton Ince in the Alex goal a virtual spectator in the first half.

Crewe, on the other hand, should have gone in at half-time with their noses in front, after both Dean Ashton and Steve Foster narrowly missed with volleys following Kenny Lunt free kicks, and Tony Warner saved well from Steve Jones and Ashton again.

Form coming into fixture

MILLWALL	CREWE
WW	LW

Warner

Lawrence Ward Nethercott Ryan

Wise Roberts Cahill Whelan

Harris Peeters

S.Jones Ashton

Rix Brammer Cochrane Lunt

Vaughan Foster Moses Wright

Ince

Juan	McCready
Hearn	Smart
Sadlier	Bankole
Gueret	Bell
P. Robinson	J. Robinson

Statistics

Season	Fixture		Fixture	Season
12	4	Shots On Target	4	12
9	1	Shots Off Target	3	16
0	0	Hit Woodwork	0	0
11	5	Caught Offside	2	4
13	4	Corners	5	13
56	19	Fouls	9	21

Matt Lawrence wins an aerial challenge.

Noel Whelan heads Millwall's late equaliser.

Lunt found space down the right hand side on plenty of occasions, but his team-mates were unable to capitalise on his hard work. Dean Ashton, called up by David Platt into the England Under-21 squad in midweek, was often the target but he was well marshalled by the Lions' defence.

Millwall showed some improvement after the break, and only a brilliant save from Ince on 54 minutes denied Tim Cahill, who met Neil Harris' cross with a firm downward header which the keeper somehow turned over the bar.

Three minutes later, however, the home side were behind after Warner needlessly charged from his goal and thumped a clearance against Ashton, who gratefully slotted the ball into an empty net for his first League goal of the season.

Juan then came on to replace the tiring Peeters, and there was a welcome return to action for Richard Sadlier with 13 minutes left.

But it was Whelan, switched up front after having started the game in midfield, who came up with the all-important leveller, glancing home Cahill's pinpoint cross right at the death.

The Lions might even have won it in injury-time, but Dennis Wise's low shot from an Andy Roberts centre lacked the power to beat Ince, and both sides had to be content with a point.

" Richard Sadlier

It's no fun sitting in the stand watching, and in fact it got to the stage for me where I couldn't do it anymore and I just used to stay at home and walk the dog instead. "

Event Line
HALF-TIME 0-0

58	🎽	⊙	Ashton (Open Play)
62	🎽	⇄	Peeters (Off) Juan (On)
77	🎽	⇄	Lawrence (Off) Sadlier (On)
77	🎽	⇄	Ryan (Off) Hearn (On)
82	🎽	⇄	Wright (Off) McCready (On)
84	🎽	☐	Ashton (Dissent)
85	🎽	☐	McCready (Ung Conduct)
86	🎽	⇄	Ashton (Off) Smart (On)
87	🎽	☐	Nethercott (Foul)
89	🎽	☐	Lunt (Foul)
90	🎽	⊙	Whelan (Open Play)

FULL-TIME 1-1

League Table	P	W	D	L	F	A	Pts
1 C Palace	3	3	0	0	7	3	9
2 Reading	3	2	1	0	7	3	7
3 Stoke City	3	2	1	0	6	2	7
4 Millwall	3	2	1	0	4	1	7
5 West Brom	3	2	0	1	6	5	6

Fixture Type: **Division One**

Date: **Tues, 26th August 2003**

Venue: **Britannia Stadium**

Attendance: **13,087**

Referee: **J.T.Winter**

STOKE CITY 0

MILLWALL 0

Form coming into fixture

STOKE CITY	MILLWALL
WWD	**WWD**

de Goey

Russell   Thomas   Williams   Hall

Eustace   Andrews   Clarke

Noel-Williams   Asaba   Greenacre

Whelan   Peeters

Juan   Hearn   Cahill   Wise

Craig   Ward   Nethercott   Roberts

Warner

Commons	Dunne
Cutler	Harris
Marteinsson	Sadler
Neal	Gueret
Iwelumo	P. Robinson

Charley Hearn fights for possession.

Statistics

Season	Fixture		Fixture	Season
25	4	Shots On Target	2	14
27	8	Shots Off Target	3	12
1	0	Hit Woodwork	0	0
12	4	Caught Offside	3	14
27	5	Corners	10	23
50	11	Fouls	15	71

Stoke City boss Tony Pulis was banished to the stands following a touchline bust-up with Mark McGhee, but nothing should detract from Millwall's excellent battling display.

That Pulis lost his rag in the dying minutes of the game was testament to the courage and conviction shown by McGhee's men in front of a vocal Britannia Stadium crowd.

There was no doubt that The Lions thoroughly deserved a share of the spoils, courtesy of a gritty, gutsy display which increasingly frustrated Stoke as the game wore on.

McGhee made a couple of surprise changes to the team held to a 1-1 draw by Crewe in the previous match, and it took The Lions a while to adjust. Not surprisingly, it was Stoke who created the better of the early chances.

Stuart Nethercott reacted quickly to clear the danger from Carl Asaba's cross in the opening minute, and Darren Ward produced an excellent block on John Eustace as Stoke started strongly.

The first clear chance of the game came on eight minutes, when Gifton Noel-Williams fired in a stinging angled drive that brought the best out of Tony Warner.

But there wasn't too much else to trouble the Millwall keeper during the first half-hour, as the visitors comfortably dealt with any potential danger and created a couple of half-chances themselves.

A delightful build-up almost paid off when Dennis Wise and

Andy Roberts gets stuck in.

Peeters set up Juan, but his drive lacked the accuracy to beat Ed de Goey in the home goal.

Noel-Williams caused an anxious moment after 28 minutes when he got the deftest of touches to a Eustace corner, only for the ball to spin wide; whilst excellent play between Juan and Whelan on the counter-attack saw the Brazilian's cross deflected for a corner.

The second period was very similar to the first, with City looking more aggressive going forward, but finding Millwall's resilient defence more than a match for their attacking intent.

Millwall provided timely reminders of their own threat as an attacking force, as Tim Cahill came agonisingly close to connecting with a neat flick from Peeters after 56 minutes and Roberts shot straight at de Goey.

Stoke were increasingly rattled by their inability to break through, and when de Goey flapped at Wise's 84th-minute corner, Whelan needed just the slightest of touches to steer the ball home, but it fell just out of reach for him to make proper contact.

That was almost too much for Stoke boss Pulis to bear, and the frustrated manager was banished to the stand seconds later when Lions boss McGhee dared to complain after Cahill was obstructed whilst clean through on goal.

It proved to be the last real noteworthy action as the game petered out in the dying stages.

Event Line		
20	☐	Roberts (Foul)
HALF-TIME 0-0		
55	⇄	Juan (Off) Dunne (On)
59	☐	Eustace (Foul)
66	⇄	Peeters (Off) Harris (On)
71	⇄	Hearn (Off) Sadlier (On)
75	⇄	Greenacre (Off) Commons (On)
85	☐	Harris (Foul)
90	☐	Whelan (Ung Conduct)
FULL-TIME 0-0		

League Table	P	W	D	L	F	A	Pts
3 Reading	4	2	2	0	7	3	8
4 Stoke City	4	2	2	0	6	2	8
5 **Millwall**	4	2	2	0	4	1	8
6 Sheff Utd	4	2	2	0	3	1	8
7 Norwich City	4	2	1	1	7	5	7

Fixture Type: **Division One**

Date: **Sat, 30th August 2003**

Venue: **The Den**

Attendance: **14,425**

Referee: **H.M.Webb**

MILLWALL 1

CRYSTAL PALACE 1

Super-sub Bob Peeters stepped off the bench to head a dramatic injury-time equaliser and maintain Millwall's unbeaten start in the First Division.

Belgian Bob used all 6ft 5in of his towering frame to head home Paul Ifill's chipped cross to break battling Palace's hearts right at the death of this ding-dong Den derby clash.

A draw was a fair result at the end of a scrappy match in which neither team got any real attacking rhythm going.

Referee Howard Webb didn't help matters by booking seven players and brandishing the red card to Palace's Tommy Black on the hour for an off-the-ball incident with Lions debutant Kevin Muscat.

All Palace could muster in the first half were a couple of long-range efforts from Shaun Derry and Black, while Millwall produced two almighty goalmouth scrambles.

The first, on 23 minutes, saw Neil Harris, Darren Ward and fit-again Ifill all blocked by Cedric Berthelin in the visiting goal.

Six minutes later, Harris's shot was deflected into the path of Noel Whelan, but he over-hit his pass to Tim Cahill and the chance went begging.

The final 15 minutes of the half were identical to the opening period of the second, with the flow of the game interrupted by booking after booking, culminating in Black's red card.

Instead of pushing forward for a winner against 10-man Palace,

Form coming into fixture

MILLWALL	C PALACE
WWDD	WWWL

Hearn	Fleming
Peeters	Cronin
Gueret	Borrowdale
P. Robinson	Soares
Livermore	Williams

Statistics

Season	Fixture		Fixture	Season
23	9	Shots On Target	4	20
16	4	Shots Off Target	3	22
0	0	Hit Woodwork	0	1
19	5	Caught Offside	4	20
31	8	Corners	5	26
89	18	Fouls	15	63

Bob Peeters celebrates his equaliser with the crowd.

Paul Ifill breaks clear of Ben Watson.

Event Line		
10		Mullins (Foul)
40		Roberts (Foul)
61		Black (Foul)
HALF-TIME 0-0		
54		Ifill (Ung Conduct)
54		Smith (Ung Conduct)
61	⮂	Whelan (Off) Hearn (On)
61		Black (Foul)
67	⊙	Watson (Direct Free Kick)
74		Cahill (Foul)
77	⮂	Craig (Off) Peeters (On)
82		Watson (Foul)
90	⊙	Peeters (Open Play)
FULL-TIME 1-1		

Millwall found themselves trailing just seven minutes later. Dennis Wise was harshly penalised for a foul on Andy Johnson in a central position just outside the 18-yard box, and up stepped 18-year-old midfielder Ben Watson to curl home a sweet free-kick which left Tony Warner rooted to the spot.

The Lions should have levelled within 60 seconds, as Wise and sub Charley Hearn combined to find Harris, who did all the hard work with a neat turn to shake off his marker, but blasted high over the bar from eight yards.

Boss Mark McGhee introduced Peeters for Tony Craig with 14 minutes to go, and the move finally kick-started The Lions into life.

Belgian striker Bob nearly scored with his first touch of the ball, only for his close-range shot to be blocked. When Wise swung over the resulting corner, Peeters sent a header narrowly wide of the mark.

Roared on by their biggest crowd of the season, Millwall piled forward with greater conviction, and when the fourth official showed five minutes of injury time, the home side stepped up another gear.

Their mounting pressure finally paid off in the 92nd minute, as Peeters stooped to knock the ball home and level the score.

The Lions still had chances to win it, with Peeters heading straight at Berthelin, Harris denied by a brilliant save from the Palace keeper, and Ifill firing over from 16 yards.

A Millwall victory would have been rough justice on The Eagles, but few could complain about McGhee's men coming away with a point after a committed performance.

League Table	P	W	D	L	F	A	Pts
6 West Ham	5	3	1	1	5	3	10
7 Sunderland	5	3	0	2	8	3	9
8 Millwall	5	2	3	0	5	2	9
9 Nottm Forest	5	3	0	2	8	6	9
10 Stoke City	5	2	2	1	6	3	8

ᴸᴸ Noel Whelan

We left it late and that is becoming a bad habit. We spoke about putting some tempo into our play, but we only showed some urgency after Palace had scored.

⁑⁑

GILLINGHAM 4

MILLWALL 3

Form coming into fixture

GILLINGHAM	MILLWALL
DWLD	WDDD

Bartram

Hope Ashby Cox

Hills Perpetuini

Spiller Shaw Southall

King Sidibe

Whelan Peeters

Cahill Wise Roberts Ifill

Craig Ward Nethercott Lawrence

Warner

Hessenthaler	Fofana
Wallace	Harris
Nosworthy	Gueret
Rose	P. Robinson
Saunders	Hearn

Statistics

Season	Fixture		Fixture	Season
28	8	Shots On Target	6	29
45	2	Shots Off Target	5	21
0	0	Hit Woodwork	0	0
22	3	Caught Offside	4	23
31	6	Corners	4	35
89	10	Fouls	19	108

Millwall's pre-match huddle.

Marlon King and Nyron Nosworthy both scored in the last eight minutes as Gillingham snatched victory from the jaws of defeat and extended their unbeaten League record against Millwall to nine matches.

It had all started so well for The Lions, who opened the scoring after just 11 minutes. Dennis Wise broke forward and found Paul Ifill, who took a couple of strides before despatching a perfectly placed 18-yard shot past home keeper Vince Bartram.

Busy midfielder Wise went close to adding a second goal a couple of minutes later, firing over with the home defence again at sixes and sevens.

Andy Roberts then hit a long range effort that was just off-target as Millwall continued to look comfortable with their lead.

But Andy Hessenthaler's side levelled with a goal on 28 minutes, Marlon King whipping in a curling cross and Mamady Sidibe stooping to send the header home.

Millwall seemed to sit back after the equaliser, and it was The Gills' greater urgency and energy that paid dividends seconds before the break, as David Perpetuini slotted a neat ball into the danger zone and former Lion Paul Shaw poked the ball past Tony Warner.

Referee Keith Hill then made a real howler, blowing his whistle for half-time some two minutes early, despite the fourth official running onto the pitch to point out his error.

Millwall boss Mark McGhee made a double substitution soon after the restart, with Neil Harris and Abou Fofana replacing Matt

Bob Peeters scores.

Event Line	
11 ⚽ Ifill (Open Play)	
28 ⚽ Sidibe (Open Play)	
43 ⚽ Shaw (Open Play)	
HALF-TIME 2-1	
52 ⇄ Lawrence (Off) Harris (On)	
52 ⇄ Whelan (Off) Fofana (On)	
61 ⚽ Peeters (Open Play)	
69 ⚽ Peeters (Open Play)	
70 ⇄ Perpetuini (Off) Hessenthaler (On)	
71 ⇄ Sidibe (Off) Wallace (On)	
72 ▢ Ashby (Foul)	
73 ⇄ Ashby (Off) Nosworthy (On)	
80 ▢ Wallace (Ung Conduct)	
80 ▢ Nethercott (Foul)	
81 ⚽ King (Open Play)	
81 ▢ Wise (Ung Conduct)	
87 ⚽ Nosworthy (Open Play)	
FULL-TIME 4-3	

League Table	P	W	D	L	F	A	Pts
6 West Ham	5	3	1	1	5	4	10
7 Sunderland	5	3	2	2	8	7	9
8 Millwall	**6**	**2**	**3**	**1**	**8**	**6**	**9**
9 Nottm Forest	5	3	0	2	8	6	9
10 Burnley	6	3	0	3	9	10	9

Lawrence and Noel Whelan. Roberts slotted in at right back, Wise moved across to central midfield and the flying Fofana filled in on the left flank.

The tactical move paid off handsomely just past the hour mark, courtesy of a sublime shot on the turn from Bob Peeters into the bottom corner of the net. Referee Hill then made another strange decision, this time booking Belgian Bob for celebrating his equaliser with the travelling Lions fans.

Peeters responded well, however, converting Millwall's third in the 69th minute after excellent work from the lively Ifill.

Harris then wasted a glorious chance to extend the lead, opting to go for glory himself, rather than square the ball for unmarked strike partner Peeters.

Gillingham started piling forward in search of an equaliser, and it took a great save on the line from Warner to keep out Rod Wallace's shot 13 minutes from time.

But there was to be no denying the Kent club, as King continued his incredible scoring run against The Lions by clipping a stunning effort beyond Warner's reach for 3-3 after 81 minutes.

And then the tables were well and truly turned in this topsy-turvy encounter, as Nosworthy toe-poked home the winner three minutes from time.

Mr Hill failed to rectify his time-keeping error, adding just three minutes on at the end, and it was too little, too late for Millwall, who headed back up the A2 with that all too familiar empty feeling.

❝ Dennis Wise

We let ourselves down with terrible defending but I still think we've got a great chance to go up with the players we've got. Bob Peeters was fantastic. He's adapted to our style right away.

❞

Fixture Type: **Division One**

Date: **Sat, 13th September 2003**

Venue: **Vicarage Road**

Attendance: **11,848**

Referee: **B.Knight**

WATFORD 3

MILLWALL 1

Neil Harris gets his foot in.

Form coming into fixture	
WATFORD	MILLWALL
LLLD	DDDL

Chamberlain

Cox Dyche Gayle Robinson

Devlin Hand Mahon Cook

Dyer Webber

Peeters Fofana

Cahill Wise Roberts Ifill

Craig Nethercott Ward Muscat

Warner

Young
Fitzgerald
Lee
Doyley
Fisken

P. Robinson
Livermore
Harris
Gueret
Hearn

Statistics

Season	Fixture		Fixture	Season
23	11	Shots On Target	4	33
30	5	Shots Off Target	1	22
0	0	Hit Woodwork	0	0
17	2	Caught Offside	4	27
25	10	Corners	4	39
72	18	Fouls	19	127

Millwall slipped to a second successive defeat after a moment of madness by Kevin Muscat handed Watford their first League win of the season.

The teams were locked at 1-1 with seconds of the first half remaining when the Australian international was shown a straight red card for appearing to stamp on Watford striker Danny Webber.

Hornets skipper Neil Cox duly tucked away the penalty into the bottom-left corner, leaving the Lions 2-1 down and facing the second half a man short, and with a task that proved beyond them.

Referee Barry Knight did little to endear himself to either team with a pedantic performance. Quite how the whistle-happy official could muster eight bookings in addition to that red card is anyone's guess. Both sets of players and supporters seemed equally perplexed by some of his fussy, irritating and at times baffling decisions; and sadly for Millwall, the rare occasion he did get it right with Muscat's dismissal proved to be the turning point.

There was little to separate the teams until then, with Watford's Bruce Dyer slamming home from close range after eight minutes following some sloppy defending, and Paul Ifill levelling on 32 minutes with a crisp finish from a Bob Peeters flick.

There were few other efforts of note in the opening half, though visiting keeper Tony Warner did well to block Webber after the lively forward had sprinted clear, and Tony Craig followed up by heading

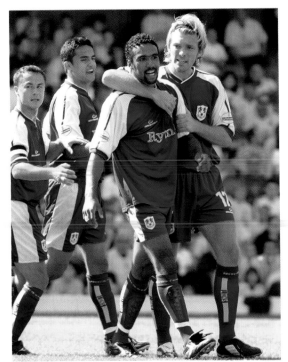

Paul Ifill celebrates his equaliser.

Event Line	
8	Dyer (Open Play)
13	Hand (Foul)
17	Craig (Foul)
20	Dyer (Foul)
27	Cox (Foul)
34	Ifill (Open Play)
45	Muscat (Violent Conduct)
45	Cox (Penalty)

HALF-TIME 2-1

46	Craig (Off) P Robinson (On)
46	Roberts (Off) Livermore (On)
53	Peeters (Foul)
61	Fofana (Off) Harris (On)
71	Ward (Foul)
76	Cook (Off) Young (On)
79	Cahill (Foul)
85	Robinson (Foul)
86	Dyer (Off) Fitzgerald (On)
90	Young (Open Play)

FULL-TIME 3-1

the return ball off the line. Ifill created a chance when he nipped in to take advantage of some hesitancy inside the Watford area and sent over a teasing cross, only for Dennis Wise's diving header to be blocked.

And then came the turning point, as Muscat went off and Cox fired the Hornets ahead with the final kick of the half.

Mark McGhee responded by bringing on Dave Livermore and Paul Robinson for Craig and the unlucky Andy Roberts, who had been one of the more impressive players in the first half. Neil Harris entered the fray on the hour mark, replacing Abou Fofana.

The Lions held their ground and had a couple of half-decent opportunities to level, though Mr Knight did his best to deny them, waving away an appeal for handball on 72 minutes, much to the fury and frustration of the visiting fans congregated behind the goal.

Tim Cahill and Harris then combined well to set up Livermore on the edge of the area, but the midfielder's rasper flew over the bar.

The Lions were attacking now, but they must have felt it just wasn't going to be their day when Cahill's spectacular overhead effort was saved on the line by home keeper Alec Chamberlain.

Watford's teenage sub Ashley Young – who looked a class act in the short time he was on the field – then put the game beyond doubt, as he marked his first-team debut by slamming home The Hornets' third goal with the final kick of the game.

League Table	P	W	D	L	F	A	Pts
10 Norwich City	6	3	1	2	9	7	10
11 Crewe	6	3	1	2	6	5	10
12 Millwall	7	2	3	2	9	9	9
13 Burnley	7	3	0	4	9	12	9
14 Gillingham	7	2	3	2	7	13	9

ⁱⁱ Mark McGhee

I feel let down by him. I knew about Kevin's history before he signed for Millwall, and we had discussions before he signed. He has cost us the game and he will be censored under club rules. He can't be doing that sort of thing.
"

Fixture Type: **Division One**

Date: **Tues, 16th September 2003**

Venue: **The Den**

Attendance: **7,855**

Referee: **P.A.Durkin**

MILLWALL 2

WIMBLEDON 0

Form coming into fixture
MILLWALL	WIMBLEDON
DDLL	LLLL

Warner

Muscat Nethercott Ward Ryan

Ifill Wise Cahill Fofana

Peeters Harris

Agyemang Nowland

Morgan Tapp Reo-Coker McAnuff

Darlington Gier Leigertwood Kamara

Banks

Whelan	Chorley
Gueret	Holdsworth
Roberts	Jarrett
Sweeney	Heald
Hearn	Holloway

Statistics

Season	Fixture		Fixture	Season
37	4	Shots On Target	4	30
32	10	Shots Off Target	2	28
0	0	Hit Woodwork	0	3
28	1	Caught Offside	4	16
43	4	Corners	1	20
137	10	Fouls	13	64

Neil Harris scored a 44th-minute penalty to send Millwall on the way to their first victory against Wimbledon in 21 years.

But The Lions were made to battle by a lively Dons outfit, and it took an injury-time effort from sub Noel Whelan to secure the points.

After successive defeats at Gillingham and Watford, winning this match was clearly the priority, rather than a top-notch performance.

Although The Lions clearly weren't firing on all cylinders, McGhee's men turned in a solid effort deserving of the three points.

Darren Ward went close to opening the scoring on 14 minutes with a looping header just over, after Harris had flicked on Dennis Wise's free kick.

Man of the match Tim Cahill provided a delightful cross for Bob Peeters seconds later, but the Belgian striker glanced his header wide.

Wimbledon's tricky midfielder Lionel Morgan caused consternation in the home defence with a sweetly struck left-foot curler that was inches over, whilst Mikele Leigertwood's fierce shot on the turn was blocked for a corner.

At the other end, Paul Ifill latched onto the loose ball after Wimbledon struggled to clear a Wise corner, but his rasping 20-yard

Neil Harris reels away in celebration after his penalty.

Abou Fofana beats Jermaine Darlington to the ball.

Event Line		
14	▯	Kamara (Foul)
23	▯	Gier (Foul)
44	⊙	Harris (Penalty)
44	⇄	Leigertwood (Off) Chorley (On)
45	▯	Nowland (Ung Conduct)
HALF-TIME 1-0		
46	▯	Tapp (Foul)
56	▯	Chorley (Foul)
71	⇄	Morgan (Off) Holdsworth (On)
75	⇄	Fofana (Off) Whelan (On)
76	⇄	Tapp (Off) Jarrett (On)
90	⊙	Whelan (Open Play)
FULL-TIME 2-0		

League Table	P	W	D	L	F	A	Pts
7 Norwich City	7	4	1	2	11	8	13
8 Sunderland	7	4	0	3	11	7	12
9 Millwall	8	3	3	2	11	9	12
10 Cardiff City	7	3	2	2	9	3	11
11 Stoke City	8	3	2	3	12	10	11

drive was well held by keeper Steve Banks. Ifill then played a key role in Millwall's opening goal, as he was sent sprawling by Banks in the area after Harris had played him clear through from a quickly taken Wise free kick.

Referee Paul Durkin pointed to the spot immediately, but Wimbledon were furious, claiming that play should have been stopped to allow them to tend to injured defender Leigertwood, who subsequently left the field seconds after Harris had slammed home the spot kick in style.

Chopper nearly turned goal provider early in the second half, wriggling his way into the danger zone and squaring for Abou Fofana, who blazed high and wide from eight yards.

A stunning dummy by Fofana enabled Ryan to charge down the left and deliver a perfect ball for Harris to flick goalwards with the outside of his left foot, only for Banks to pluck the ball out as it was heading for the top corner.

Harris was denied again on 69 minutes when his header smacked the woodwork, and Cahill headed the follow-up over from six yards.

Tony Warner, who had been a virtual spectator until then, was increasingly called into action as the second half wore on and The Dons pushed forward in an all-or-nothing bid to salvage something from the game.

But it was Lions sub Whelan who made the points safe deep into injury-time. After Ifill did well to win possession on the right, Cahill charged and powered forward before delivering a perfectly weighted pass that Whelan swept home from eight yards.

❝ Theo Paphitis

The club have had to come to terms with the fact that we have lost a prized asset in Richard Sadlier, who has been forced to retire. He would have been a major contributor towards our promotion efforts.
❞

❝ Neil Harris

It's been seven games and it's very important to get off the mark. The pressure is huge as a centre forward, especially when I've scored goals throughout my career and the team's struggling. It helps the team out and gives my own confidence a tremendous boost.
❞

Fixture Type: **Division One**

Date: **Sat, 20th September 2003**

Venue: **The Den**

Attendance: **9,262**

Referee: **P.J.Prosser**

MILLWALL 2

WALSALL 1

Form coming into fixture

MILLWALL	WALSALL
DLLW	**LDLL**

Warner

Muscat Nethercott Ward Ryan

Ifill Wise Cahill Livermore

Peeters Harris

Leitao Burton

Birch Corica Osborn Samways

Wrack Ritchie Hay Bazeley

Walker

Dunne	Lawrence
Whelan	Emblen
Gueret	Oakes
Roberts	Kerr
Hearn	Fryatt

Statistics

Season	Fixture		Fixture	Season
45	8	Shots On Target	2	33
37	5	Shots Off Target	6	36
0	0	Hit Woodwork	0	1
31	3	Caught Offside	2	20
46	3	Corners	3	38
153	16	Fouls	15	95

Neil Harris struck a 79th-minute penalty winner as plucky Millwall battled back to secure a second successive win, at the expense of struggling Walsall.

The game didn't start too brightly for The Lions, however, as they went a goal down after five minutes.

Steve Corica split a static home defence with a neatly flicked through-ball to Deon Burton, who was clumsily hauled down by keeper Tony Warner. Referee Phil Prosser brandished the first of an incredible nine yellow cards, and Corica sent the keeper the wrong way to execute a perfect penalty.

Dennis Wise dragged a 20-yarder just wide after good work from Paul Ifill, and in the 15th minute, Darren Ward's backward header from Wise's free kick floated past Walker for Millwall's leveller.

Ifill's terrific 19th-minute pass found Harris, who in turn played a

Darren Ward and Neil Harris celebrate the winner.

Harris holds off a challenge.

perfect return ball for the winger, but Ifill's 16-yard rocket went straight into the arms of Walker.

Kevin Muscat was denied by the woodwork on 29 minutes with a curling cross-shot, Walker just getting a hand to push the ball out and then making a brilliant save to deny Harris from the rebound.

Walsall were also creating chances of their own, as Gary Birch headed over from Darren Bazeley's cross, Burton's hooked effort flashed inches wide and Vinny Samways' left-foot free kick curled past the post with Warner stranded.

But The Lions totally dominated proceedings after the break.

Harris, Dave Livermore – making his first start of the season in place of the injured Abou Fofana – and Tim Cahill all went close, as Millwall continued to prise and probe the visiting defence in search of a second goal.

Bob Peeters was inches away from connecting with a Cahill pull-back with the goal at his mercy, and when Ifill delayed too long before pulling the trigger six yards out, it looked as if Millwall's afternoon was going to end in frustration.

But then, with 11 minutes remaining, Ifill was sent tumbling by the faintest of touches from Walsall sub Stefan Oakes, and Chopper stepped up to drill the resulting penalty past Walker.

Millwall could have added a third after 85 minutes when Alan Dunne's long ball found fellow sub Noel Whelan, who delivered a perfect pass into the box for Chopper, only for the striker to mis-hit his shot from just four yards out.

League Table	P	W	D	L	F	A	Pts
4 West Ham	8	5	1	2	9	12	16
5 Nottm Forest	8	5	0	3	15	10	15
6 Millwall	**9**	**4**	**3**	**2**	**13**	**10**	**15**
7 Reading	8	4	2	2	13	7	14
8 Norwich City	8	4	2	2	12	9	14

❦ Mark McGhee

Since the start of the season it's been evident that the squad is still short of cover, which was best demonstrated by Paul Ifill's absence for four games of which we won only one. I remain determined to strengthen, but in the meantime I'm content that the group of players who are available are giving me the maximum effort they can.

"

Fixture Type: **Division One**

Date: **Sun, 28th September 2003**

Venue: **Upton Park**

Attendance: **31,626**

Referee: **M.R.Halsey**

WEST HAM UNITED 1

MILLWALL 1

Form coming into fixture
WEST HAM UTD	MILLWALL
WWWL	LLWW

James

Repka   Pearce   Dailly   Quinn

Horlock   Lee   Etherington

Defoe   Connolly   Mellor

Peeters   Ifill

Livermore   Wise   Roberts   Cahill

Craig   Ward   Nethercott   Dunne

Warner

Alexandersson	Lawrence
Ferdinand	Harris
Bywater	Gueret
Kilgallon	Hearn
Garcia	Whelan

Statistics

Season	Fixture		Fixture	Season
57	6	Shots On Target	6	51
39	3	Shots Off Target	2	39
3	1	Hit Woodwork	1	1
33	5	Caught Offside	2	33
49	5	Corners	4	50
110	14	Fouls	12	165

Tim Cahill heads in the equaliser.

Tim Cahill sent Millwall's army of supporters into ecstasy with a 73rd-minute goal to earn a draw in a pulsating Upton Park clash.

Pint-sized striker David Connolly had fired the Hammers into a 23rd-minute lead, and it looked as if a combination of woodwork and the excellent form of keeper David James was going to deny Mark McGhee's men a thoroughly deserved share of the spoils.

But roared on by 2,543 fans, Lions livewire Paul Ifill made space on the right and sent over a perfect cross which Cahill met with a downward header past the outstretched hands of James.

Millwall had a glorious chance in the eighth minute, when Bob Peeters exchanged passes with Ifill and found Cahill rushing in unmarked from 12 yards, but James reacted superbly to deflect his goalbound effort wide with an outstretched leg.

Tony Warner then comfortably held efforts from Neil Mellor, Matthew Etherington and Connolly, who really should have done better with a free header eight yards out.

But the little frontman made no mistake after 25 minutes, when he latched onto Rob Lee's through-ball, shrugged off the attention of Darren Ward and buried his shot into the bottom-right corner.

Millwall came back strongly, Ian Pearce heading Tony Craig's cross inches over and James holding Andy Roberts's dinked header following a fine Dave Livermore delivery.

Tony Craig gets past Niclas Alexandersson's challenge.

It took a perfectly timed tackle from Thomas Repka to deny the outstanding Ifill as the lively Lion sprinted into the box on 35 minutes, and Cahill saw his 43rd-minute header from a Dennis Wise free kick held on the line by James.

McGhee made a couple of changes at the break, introducing Neil Harris for Roberts and calling on the experienced Matt Lawrence to replace right back Alan Dunne.

But the duo had barely had time to get a touch of the ball when Jermain Defoe's volley was deflected straight into Etherington's path and he blasted a shot against the far post.

Millwall's reaction was exactly as you would expect, and James was forced into action on 54 minutes, holding Cahill's first-timer from 20 yards at the second attempt.

Harris went close five minutes later with an exquisite piece of skill, taking the ball on his chest, flicking it up with his knee and then letting fly with a dipping volley that dropped a foot over the bar.

Ifill then picked up Ward's long ball and thumped an angled drive off the woodwork on 67 minutes, before Cahill levelled the score with his cracking header.

Millwall looked the more likely side to grab a late second goal, as Peeters had a header cleared off the line and Harris saw his 85th-minute snap shot saved by the busy James.

West Ham did, however, have a great chance to nick victory right at the death, but Defoe was a tad greedy yet again, as he went for goal with Connolly in a far better position and dragged his shot wide.

Event Line			
25	⚽		Connolly (Open Play)
39		☐	Craig (Foul)
43		☐	Connolly (Ung Conduct)
45		☐	Peeters (Foul)
HALF-TIME 1-0			
46	⮂		Mellor (Off) Alexandersson (On)
46	⮂		Dunne (Off) Lawrence (On)
46	⮂		Roberts (Off) Harris (On)
73	⚽		Cahill (Open Play)
80	⮂		Pearce (Off) Ferdinand (On)
89		☐	Quinn (Foul)
FULL-TIME 1-1			

League Table	P	W	D	L	F	A	Pts
6 Sunderland	9	5	1	3	14	8	16
7 Nottm Forest	9	5	1	3	16	11	16
8 Millwall	**10**	**4**	**4**	**2**	**14**	**11**	**16**
9 Cardiff	9	4	2	3	19	12	14
10 Reading	9	4	2	3	13	9	14

WEST BROMWICH ALBION 2

MILLWALL 1

Form coming into fixture
WEST BROM	MILLWALL
WLDW	LWWD

Hoult

Gregan Gaardsoe Gilchrist

Haas Clement

Koumas O'Connor Johnson

Dobie Hulse

Peeters Harris

Livermore Ifill

Cahill Wise

Craig Lawrence

Ward Nethercott

Warner

Berthe	Whelan
Dichio	P. Robinson
Murphy	Gueret
Sakiri	Dunne
Hughes	Roberts

Statistics

Season	Fixture		Fixture	Season
66	10	Shots On Target	4	55
55	5	Shots Off Target	1	40
4	0	Hit Woodwork	0	1
35	3	Caught Offside	4	37
60	2	Corners	1	51
134	15	Fouls	16	181

Jason Koumas and Scott Dobie struck twice in the opening 24 minutes to send Millwall spinning to defeat at The Hawthorns.

Midfielder Koumas bagged a fifth-minute wonder strike for the Baggies, before Dobie added a second killer goal 19 minutes later.

Although Stuart Nethercott reduced the arrears on the stroke of half-time, Mark McGhee's gutsy Lions could not turn a vastly improved second half display into an equalising goal.

Millwall were caught napping twice in 24 costly opening minutes. After just five, Jason Koumas capitalised on some truly woeful marking to curl a 20-yarder past stranded Lions' keeper Tony Warner.

Despite Koumas's premature departure through injury five minutes later, West Brom maintained their shape, composure and total control of affairs for long periods of the opening half.

Andy Johnson went close to adding a second goal on 21 minutes, intercepting a poor Nethercott pass intended for Tim Cahill, but he shot straight at Warner with the goal at his mercy.

Matt Lawrence attempts a clearance.

The goalmouth scramble leading to Stuart Nethercott's goal.

There was to be no such let-off again three minutes later when another Nethercott error led to The Baggies' second goal. Faced with a seemingly straight forward clearance, Nethers tried to head clear, only for the ball to bounce invitingly for striker Dobie, who made no mistake with a looping header past Warner.

That should have been that, but this is Millwall, and you should always expect the unexpected. Straight from the restart, Neil Harris sidefooted the ball into the arms of home keeper Russell Hoult with the Baggies' rearguard in snooze land.

Gary Megson's men reacted immediately and Bernt Haas forced Warner into a fine save, before Tony Craig finally scrambled clear.

But the home side were made to pay dearly for a vital lapse in concentration seconds before the break, when Harris picked up a neat Bob Peeters flick and saw his shot deflected behind by keeper Hoult. Dennis Wise curled in the resulting corner kick, and although Nethercott's header was blocked, the ball fell back to the Lions defender, who blasted it over the line from close range.

Boss McGhee acted on this, and in a bid to try and grab all three points sacrificed left-back Tony Craig for striker Noel Whelan.

There is no doubt that The Lions looked far more cohesive and composed during the second half, but were let down by their distribution into the final third of the field.

Millwall's best chance of salvaging a point from the match came eight minutes from time, when Ifill's low drive was comfortably dealt with by Hoult, whilst at the other end Hulse was denied by Warner as The Baggies briefly threatened to nick a third goal.

Event Line

Time			Event
5	⚽	⊙	Koumas (Open Play)
10	⚽	⇄	Koumas (Off) Berthe (On)
24	⚽	⊙	Dobie (Open Play)
34	⚽	▢	O'Connor (Foul)
45	🏆	⊙	Nethercott (Corner)
HALF-TIME 2-1			
46	🏆	⇄	Craig (Off) Whelan (On)
63	⚽	▢	Gregan (Foul)
66	🏆	⇄	Harris (Off) P Robinson (On)
66	🏆	▢	Lawrence (Ung Conduct)
80	⚽	⇄	Dobie (Off) Dichio (On)
84	🏆	▢	Peeters (Ung Conduct)
FULL-TIME 2-1			

League Table	P	W	D	L	F	A	Pts
6 West Ham	9	5	2	2	10	6	17
7 Nottm Forest	9	5	1	3	16	11	16
8 Millwall	**11**	**4**	**4**	**3**	**15**	**13**	**16**
9 Cardiff	10	4	3	3	19	12	15
10 Reading	10	4	2	4	14	11	14

Fixture Type: **Division One**

Date: **Sat, 4th October 2003**

Venue: **The Den**

Attendance: **9,849**

Referee: **P.J.Joslin**

MILLWALL 2

COVENTRY CITY 1

Form coming into fixture

MILLWALL	COVENTRY CITY
WWDL	LWDW

```
                Warner

Lawrence  P. Robinson  Ward   Craig

  Ifill    Wise   Cahill  Livermore

       Whelan   Peeters

        Adebola  Morrell

Jorgensen                    Barrett
      McAllister   Safri

Staunton                    Whing
       Shaw     Konjic

          Shearer
```

Fofana	Joachim
Harris	Davenport
Roberts	Warnock
Gueret	Arphexad
Nethercott	Mansouri

Statistics

Season	Fixture		Fixture	Season
59	4	Shots On Target	6	85
42	2	Shots Off Target	3	76
1	0	Hit Woodwork	1	3
46	9	Caught Offside	2	25
54	3	Corners	6	73
202	21	Fouls	10	112

Paul Ifill fires Millwall in front.

Substitute Neil Harris was the hero after firing a late winner – but Millwall's victory was soured by Tim Cahill's injury-time sending off for a second yellow card.

Paul Ifill has opened The Lions' account on 62 minutes, only for Steve Staunton to haul Coventry level with a hotly disputed penalty.

But it was Chopper who picked the perfect time to score his first goal from open play this season, stealing the points.

The Lions had their tails up and looked good to push on and get a third goal, before referee Phil Joslin to brandished a second yellow card to Cahill for a 90th-minute challenge on Calum Davenport.

That set up a nail-biting finale, which saw Mark McGhee's ten men battle to deny the Sky Blues an equalising goal.

Three points was ultimately no more than Millwall deserved as reward for a vibrant second-half display, in which they shook off the lethargy of a woeful opening 45 minutes to dominate proceedings.

However, there is no doubt that the home goal led a charmed life during the early exchanges, as Coventry did everything but score.

Player-manager Gary McAllister smacked the woodwork on 18 minutes following a sweeping move, before he was denied again, this time by keeper Tony Warner's excellent 26th-minute tip over.

Millwall rarely threatened the visiting goal prior to the break, with Dave Livermore's 30-yard drive, which flashed wide on the half-hour mark, the only noteworthy effort.

In fact, their frustrations boiled over when Noel Whelan and

Neil Harris holds off Steve Staunton to score the winner.

	Event Line
25	Safri (Foul)
37	Shaw (Foul)
HALF-TIME 0-0	
54	Cahill (Foul)
63	Ifill (Open Play)
67	Barrett (Off) Joachim (On)
68	Whing (Foul)
72	Konjic (Off) Davenport (On)
72	Staunton (Penalty)
74	Morrell (Foul)
77	Livermore (Off) Fofana (On)
78	Peeters (Off) Harris (On)
85	Harris (Open Play)
86	Ifill (Off) Roberts (On)
90	Cahill (Foul)
90	Adebola (Off) Warnock (On)
FULL-TIME 2-1	

Cahill were involved in an unnecessary exchange, before skipper Dennis Wise intervened and sensibly calmed the situation.

It was boss McGhee's turn to pick his words carefully at the break, and whatever he said clearly had the desired effect as The Lions came out looking a different proposition.

Whelan was thwarted twice in quick succession, with a first-time shot pushed away by keeper Shearer on 56 minutes, and then seeing his 57th-minute effort blocked on the line.

Millwall's pressure finally paid off five minutes later when Ifill lashed a left-foot shot home from six yards at the second attempt after Coventry failed to clear Tony Craig's long throw.

Less than ten minutes later, the Sky Blues battled back to level the scores. Matt Lawrence was penalised for a foul on Staunton, and the defender stepped up to slot home the resulting spot-kick.

McGhee responded by bringing on Abou Fofana and Harris for Peeters and Livermore, and the move paid off handsomely as The Lions used their pace and mobility to stretch the visiting defence.

There were barely five minutes remaining when Coventry finally crumbled – Chopper chested down Lawrence's pass from the left, took his time before calmly slotting home the winner.

Cahill's untimely dismissal set up a nervy finale, but The Lions defence held firm for a third successive home win to stay in the promotion mix.

League Table	P	W	D	L	F	A	Pts
5 Wigan	11	6	4	1	15	7	22
6 Norwich	11	6	3	2	17	12	21
7 Millwall	12	5	4	3	17	14	19
8 Burnley	12	5	2	5	19	19	17
9 Nottm Forest	11	5	1	5	17	14	16

❝ Mark McGhee

**We huffed and puffed, but there was no real quality there.
I was waiting for some sort of shape to emerge throughout the game.**

❞

❝ Paul Ifill

We are playing nowhere near the level we are capable of and at the moment are reaching only 65 per cent – but there is plenty more to come from us. We have been missing that little spark and maybe this result will give us the lift we need.

❞

ROTHERHAM UNITED 0

MILLWALL 0

Form coming into fixture

ROTHERHAM UTD	MILLWALL
LDWL	WDLW

Pollitt

Swailes McIntosh
Scott   Minto

Baudet Talbot
Sedgwick   Warne

Butler Byfield

Peeters Whelan

Livermore   Ifill
Cahill Wise

Craig   Muscat
Ward P. Robinson

Warner

Monkhouse   Harris
Hurst   Fofana
Montgomery   Gueret
R.Barker   Lawrence
Robins   Nethercott

Statistics

Season	Fixture		Fixture	Season
65	5	Shots On Target	2	61
53	6	Shots Off Target	5	47
0	0	Hit Woodwork	0	1
31	2	Caught Offside	1	47
61	5	Corners	4	58
177	10	Fouls	15	217

Millwall ground out what could prove to be a valuable awayday point at struggling Rotherham United, but the match itself proved to be an instantly forgettable spectacle.

A point apiece was just about right, as both teams huffed and puffed in equal measure, but were also unable to find the spark of creativity needed to break the deadlock in this draw.

In a dour opening half, United's best effort came three minutes before the break, when Butler's effort to went a foot over the bar.

At the other end of the field, Bob Peeters thought he had given

Tony Warner denies Martin Butler.

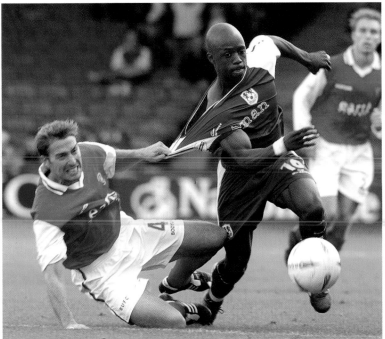
Rob Scott holds back Abou Fofana.

Millwall an early lead with a close-range drive, only for his effort to be ruled out for offside.

The big Belgian went close again on 37 minutes, but this time his lob was cleared off the line by Scott Minto.

The Lions had keeper Tony Warner to thank for enabling them to go in at the break on level terms with a solid punch to clear Julian Baudet's 44th-minute header.

Unfortunately, the second half was not much better than the first, and home supporters were streaming out of the ground long before the end rather than endure Rotherham's fourth goalless draw at Millmoor in their last six outings.

United striker Darren Byfield's low drive was smartly stopped by Warner five minutes after the restart, but it was only in the last 10 minutes, with the additional pace of substitutes Neil Harris and Abou Fofana, that Millwall really threatened.

Ifill was denied by the bravery of Pollitt, who retrieved the ball from the winger's feet as he broke into the danger zone.

Fofana's toe-poke was also saved by the keeper in the dying seconds, but a late winner would have been rough justice on Ronnie Moore's battlers.

44 Darren Ward

It's a decent squad with a lot of ability. But we haven't really shown it yet and we'd better hurry up because there's nearly a third of the season gone.
77

Event Line			
39			Wise (Foul)
HALF-TIME 0-0			
62			Peeters (Off) Harris (On)
64			Cahill (Ung Conduct)
66			Livermore (Off) Fofana (On)
79			Warne (Off) Monkhouse (On)
86			Baudet (Off) Hurst (On)
FULL-TIME 0-0			

League Table	P	W	D	L	F	A	Pts
5 Sunderland	11	7	1	3	18	10	22
6 Norwich	11	6	3	2	17	12	21
7 Millwall	**13**	**5**	**5**	**3**	**17**	**14**	**20**
8 Burnley	12	5	2	5	19	19	17
9 Ipswich	12	5	2	5	17	17	17

MILLWALL 0

PRESTON NORTH END 1

PRESTON NORTH END FC

Form coming into fixture

MILLWALL	PRESTON NE
DLWD	WLWW

Warner

P. Robinson   Roberts   Ward

Muscat   Wise   Cahill   Livermore   Dunne

Ifill   Harris

Fuller   Cresswell

Keane   O'Neil   McKenna

Lewis   Alexander

Broomes   Lucketti   Jackson

Gould

Whelan	Cartwright
Nethercott	Edwards
Peeters	Davis
Gueret	Lonergan
Fofana	Healy

Statistics

Season	Fixture		Fixture	Season
61	0	Shots On Target	6	92
50	3	Shots Off Target	5	83
1	0	Hit Woodwork	0	1
48	1	Caught Offside	5	45
62	4	Corners	2	75
229	12	Fouls	12	163

Preston's Paul McKenna bagged a 51st-minute winner, as the lacklustre Lions slipped to their first home League defeat of the season.

It was a night of disappointment for the home supporters, who watched the match with increasing frustration at Millwall's inability to pressurise the Preston defence.

Den boss Mark McGhee had opted for a 3-5-2 formation to try and match the pace and power of Craig Brown's fellow high-fliers.

But it was Preston who looked more comfortable, and once the deadlock was broken after the break they looked unlikely to surrender their lead.

There were barely two minutes on the clock when Graham Alexander tried his luck with a 35-yarder, which Tony Warner dealt with comfortably.

Richard Cresswell twice went close, heading wide from just six yards and then being denied by a great Darren Ward block tackle.

Ricardo Fuller, who led the front line superbly, forced Warner into another save on 14 minutes as Preston continued to test the home defence.

Neil Harris turns Chris Lucketti.

Paul Ifill fires just wide.

Paul Ifill had Millwall's first real chance of the night after 24 minutes, but ballooned his effort over the bar. Iffs, who partnered Neil Harris up front, should have put the home side ahead two minutes later, but fired wide of the mark from 15 yards.

Cresswell was unlucky with a dipping 20-yard volley on the half-hour mark and then Eddie Lewis dragged a shot into the side netting as Preston kept the pressure on.

After half-time, Millwall continued to struggle against a well-organised, enterprising North End outfit. It took just six minutes from the restart for McKenna to slam home the all-important winner, converting from close-range after a powerful run and pass from Fuller.

Millwall's best chance of levelling came within two minutes of going behind, but Ifill again shot wide.

Despite the introduction of Noel Whelan and then Bob Peeters, The Lions just couldn't get any real rhythm to their play, and as the second half progressed, so did the yellow card count with four players finding their way into referee Trevor Parkes' book.

Preston threatened again with McKenna's effort flying past the post, Paul Robinson nearly turning the ball into his own net and then Alexander was denied by Warner as the visitors finished strongly.

The major drama of the night, however, occured in the boardroom after the final whistle as Mark McGhee's three year managerial reign came to an end.

League Table	P	W	D	L	F	A	Pts
6 Norwich	11	6	3	2	17	12	21
7 Ipswich	13	6	2	5	23	18	20
8 Millwall	**14**	**5**	**5**	**4**	**17**	**15**	**20**
9 Preston	12	6	1	5	16	13	19
10 Reading	12	5	3	4	18	14	18

‟ Theo Paphitis

I had a long discussion with Mark after the game and it was felt by both of us that we should part company by mutual consent. It was very amicable and we move on. Expectations here have always been high and I think it was apparent that results and performances have not gone as we would have liked in the first two months of the season.

”

MILLWALL 2

SHEFFIELD UNITED 0

Form coming into fixture

MILLWALL	SHEFF UTD
LWDL	WWLW

Warner	
P. Robinson D. Ward	
Muscat	Ryan
Roberts Livermore	
Ifill	Fofana
Peeters Harris	

M. Ward

Montgomery Ndlovu

McCall Tonge Brown

Whitlow Kozluk
Morgan Jagielka

Gerrard

Gueret	Armstrong
Nethercott	Rankine
Wise	Allison
Braniff	Lester
Whelan	Peschisolido

Ray Wilkins looks on from the sidelines

Second-half goals from Neil Harris and Paul Ifill did the damage, as nine-man Millwall held on for an outstanding victory against top of the table United, in a dramatic Den encounter.

The Lions were in complete control and cruising to three morale-boosting points courtesy of Chopper's 51st-minute penalty and an angled drive by Iffs on 65 minutes.

But then referee Rob Styles tarnished what had promised to be a memorable afternoon for Lions' new caretaker-manager Dennis Wise, brandishing red cards to Dave Livermore and then Wise himself, just four minutes after he had come on as a sub for Abou Fofana.

Bob Peeters and Harris both went close as Millwall set their attacking stall out from the off. Chopper in particular, was unlucky with a stunning left-foot drive that flashed inches wide after a fine build-up involving Robbie Ryan and Peeters.

Ifill shot wide, Peeters' header was blocked for a corner and the Belgian again went close, as the Lions carved out a stack of chances.

At the other end, Mike Whitlow headed Michael Tonge's 16th-minute corner over, with United's only real effort of the first half.

In fact, it took until the 47th-minute for Tony Warner to make his first save of the game - and what a vital one it was too – tipping Michael Brown's close-range volley over the bar for a corner.

But four minutes later The Lions were ahead when Abou picked up a Harris pass and sprinted into the area, only to be sent tumbling

Statistics

Season	Fixture		Fixture	Season
67	6	Shots On Target	8	79
57	7	Shots Off Target	4	67
1	0	Hit Woodwork	0	2
54	6	Caught Offside	1	26
72	10	Corners	3	61
247	18	Fouls	16	155

Dennis Wise sees red.

Event Line	
27	Livermore (Foul)
29	Muscat (Foul)
35	Fofana (Foul)
HALF-TIME 0-0	
51	Harris (Penalty)
58	McCall (Off) Peschisolido (On)
66	Ifill (Corner)
68	Whitlow (Foul)
69	Montgomery (Off) Armstrong (On)
69	Ward (Off) Allison (On)
81	Livermore (Time Wasting)
83	Fofana (Off) Wise (On)
84	Allison (Foul)
84	Tonge (Foul)
86	Peeters (Off) Whelan (On)
87	Wise (Foul)
FULL-TIME 2-0	

League Table	P	W	D	L	F	A	Pts
5 West Ham	13	7	4	2	17	9	25
6 Ipswich	14	7	2	5	24	18	23
7 Millwall	**15**	**6**	**5**	**4**	**19**	**15**	**23**
8 Norwich	13	6	4	3	18	14	22
9 Reading	13	6	3	4	21	16	21

by Rob Kozluk. Chopper stepped up to smash a right-foot penalty past Paul Gerrard in the United goal.

The little winger appeared to have been tripped in the area just two minutes later, but the referee waved play on.

Fofana then sent in a fine free-kick which Peeters met with a diving header forcing Gerrard to brilliantly tip wide.

But there was to be no denying the rampant Lions a second goal, and when United only half-cleared Andy Roberts' corner, Ifill lashed home an angled drive at the second attempt.

It was all Millwall, with Ifill and Muscat both producing solo runs that deserved a goal, as Wise's side continued to dominate.

United, with all three substitues on in a bid to claw their way back into the game, came close to doing just that when sub Wayne Allison's 78th-minute header from a Peter Ndlovu cross was just a whisker away from finding the net.

They were given a man-advantage when Livers picked up his second yellow card of the game for time-wasting on 81 minutes, and another for the final two minutes, when Wise was also shown red following a crunching tackle on Chris Armstrong.

But other than a quickly-taken free-kick from Michael Brown that Warner held comfortably, United were unable to capitalise on their numerical advantage and Millwall resolutely held on for three thoroughly deserved points.

❝ Dennis Wise

For the first 80 minutes the lads were fantastic. We deserved to win and I could praise the whole team, but in particular, Andy Roberts, Dave Livermore and Neil Harris were outstanding.

❞

BURNLEY 1

MILLWALL 1

Form coming into fixture

BURNLEY	MILLWALL
DWLD	**WDLW**

Jensen

West Gnohere Branch Camara

Chadwick Weller Chaplow

Blake
I. Moore Facey

Peeters Harris

Sweeney Ifill
Livermore Roberts

Ryan Muscat
Ward P. Robinson

Warner

⚽ Grant	Whelan ⚽
Farrelly	Braniff
Roche	Gueret
Pilkington	Lawrence
O'Neill	Wise

Statistics

Season	Fixture		Fixture	Season
96	6	Shots On Target	5	72
78	7	Shots Off Target	6	63
3	0	Hit Woodwork	1	2
51	3	Caught Offside	5	59
86	9	Corners	6	78
188	8	Fouls	19	266

Noel Whelan maintained Dennis Wise's unbeaten start as caretaker Millwall manager with a goal in this entertaining Turf Moor encounter – but an excellent result was marred by a first-half injury to striker Neil Harris.

Chopper fell awkwardly when trying to connect with a Paul Ifill cross midway through the first half, and was clearly in considerable discomfort when he eventually left the field after lengthy treatment.

Caretaker-boss Wise made one change to the team that had beaten Sheffield United the previous weekend, drafting Scottish U21 winger Peter Sweeney into the starting line-up in place of Abou Fofana, who was on international duty with the Ivory Coast.

But it was Burnley who were thrown into total disarray after just three minutes, with the withdrawal of Paul Weller through injury.

Weller was replaced in midfield by Tony Grant, having seemingly suffered a recurrence of the ankle problem that had put his participation in this game in doubt.

Millwall looked to take advantage of Burnley's mishap, and twice went close through Bob Peeters.

The big Belgian perhaps should have done better on 16 minutes with a volley that lacked power and was comfortably held by Brian Jensen in the home goal.

But it took a superlative save from the keeper to deny Peeters three minutes later, somehow tipping his close-range shot from a

Neil Harris in action before his injury.

Peter Sweeney takes control.

Harris cross around the post for a corner. Just as The Lions were starting to take charge, Chopper sustained his injury and was replaced by Whelan. It was now Burnley turning the screw as Wise's men re-grouped.

Delroy Facey's effort was blocked by Darren Ward after good work from Robbie Blake, Mo Camara crossed for Dean West to head wide, and Luke Chadwick shot straight at Tony Warner in the space of three minutes.

However, Ifill's powerful drive whistled inches wide whilst Peeters' strike was kept out by another point-blank stop from Jensen as Millwall finished the half strongly.

It took just eight minutes after the break for The Lions to finally find a way past Jensen courtesy of sub Whelan's header from a Peeters flick-on.

The lead lasted just seven minutes as Ian Moore stabbed home virtually on the goal line after the visitors failed to clear Facey's low drive.

Loan striker Facey tried his luck from distance three times in quick succession, whilst at the other end Kevin Braniff, a 62nd-minute sub for Peeters, clipped the woodwork and was unlucky with another effort that flashed over the bar.

Burnley were denied a late winner by the smart reflexes of Warner, who blocked Blake's goal-bound drive to ensure that the spoils were shared between these teams for a fourth successive time.

❦ Dennis Wise

I was very disappointed that we didn't win the game, because we could easily have been three goals up at half-time. Losing Chopper is a big blow. I asked him to play in a different position and it suited him. He was causing people all sorts of problems, and his injury unsettled things for 15 or 20 minutes while we sorted it out. Before that, we were in full flow and Chopper was looking like a real goalscorer.

""

MILLWALL 1

NOTTINGHAM FOREST 0

Substitute Kevin Braniff picked the perfect time to score his first ever League goal, with a winner deep into first-half injury time to secure three priceless points for Millwall.

But The Lions' victory was marred by an injury to striker Noel Whelan, who limped off five minutes before the break, plus another booking for fellow striker Bob Peeters, his fifth of the season.

Whilst it may not have been the most attractive of performances, few could doubt the commitment of Dennis Wise's young charges as they dug deep to repel a late Forest onslaught.

Caretaker-boss Wise again relegated himself to the subs' bench, welcoming Tim Cahill back in place of the suspended Dave Livermore, plus Abou Fofana for the injured Paul Ifill.

Fellow youngster Peter Sweeney, making his first home start of the campaign, nearly fired Millwall ahead after just 57 seconds, but keeper Darren Ward held his low drive at the second attempt.

When the Forest defence could only half-clear Kevin Muscat's free-kick four minutes later, Cahill retrieved the ball and worked an opening before curling a cross just too high for Peeters.

It was Paul Hart's side who then began to find their rhythm, and

Form coming into fixture

MILLWALL	NOTTM F
DLWD	DWDW

Warner

Muscat   P. Robinson   Ward   Ryan

Sweeney   Roberts   Cahill   Fofana

Whelan   Peeters

Taylor   Harewood

Reid   Jess   Williams   Stewart

Morgan   Walker   Thompson   Louis-Jean

Ward

Braniff	Bopp
Hearn	Robertson
Gueret	McPhail
Lawrence	Roche
Wise	Gunnarsson

Statistics

Season	Fixture		Fixture	Season
80	8	Shots On Target	4	98
66	3	Shots Off Target	5	82
2	0	Hit Woodwork	0	1
60	1	Caught Offside	6	51
83	5	Corners	2	118
284	18	Fouls	16	180

Bob Peeters controls the ball.

Kevin Braniff opens his League account.

Event Line		
43		Whelan (Off) Braniff (On)
45		Braniff (Open Play)
HALF-TIME 1-0		
49		Louis-Jean (Foul)
67		Fofana (Off) Hearn (On)
74		Jess (Off) Bopp (On)
77		Louis-Jean (Off) Robertson (On)
81		Williams (Off) McPhail (On)
84		Peeters (Foul)
85		Bopp (Dissent)
FULL-TIME 1-0		

League Table	P	W	D	L	F	A	Pts
6 West Ham	16	7	7	2	19	11	28
7 Ipswich	17	8	3	6	32	26	27
8 Millwall	17	7	6	4	21	16	27
9 Cardiff	16	6	6	4	27	16	24
10 Nottm Forest	16	7	3	6	28	19	24

Eoin Jess really should have done better on ten minutes when Marlon Harewood and Gareth Taylor combined to set the midfielder up, but he drove over from 20 yards with only Tony Warner to beat.

The keeper then had to be at his best twice in quick succession, using his body to block Taylor's effort on the goalline, before somehow scooping away the striker's goalbound header.

Whelan's early departure through injury paved the way for 20-year-old Braniff to enter the fray. Within two minutes he had a goal disallowed after Abou was penalised for handball, but the Northern Ireland U21 international was not to be denied. Deep into injury-time, he rose majestically to meet Sweeney's pinpoint cross and send a glancing header past Ward's outstretched hands.

Millwall were denied a penalty seconds after the restart, when Louis-Jean clearly pulled Fofana back as he sprinted into the area. The Forest man was booked and The Lions awarded a free-kick inches outside the danger zone, which sadly came to nothing.

Scoring chances were few and far between during the second period, with Peeters crashing his shot over on 62 minutes and Harewood's fiercely struck effort held by Warner seven minutes later.

Forest appealed for a penalty in the dying seconds when Cahill handled – but what goes around comes around. Last season the hand of David Johnson proved decisive when he controlled the ball with his hand before firing into the net during a 2-1 Forest win. This time, the hand of fate intervened – and The Lions were more than grateful to accept the present!

" Ray Wilkins

It wasn't the swashbuckling performance we had against Sheffield United, but against a side like Forest, who are a good passing team, the lads showed great discipline throughout the whole side, and I thought the young guys did particularly well.

"

" Kevin Braniff

It was a brilliant feeling. I was waiting for so long to score a goal and now it's come I really am over the moon. The last goal I scored for the first team was at Brighton and my second goal has been some time coming.

"

Fixture Type: **Division One**

Date: **Sat, 8th November 2003**

Venue: **Carrow Road**

Attendance: **16,423**

Referee: **M.Clattenburg**

NORWICH CITY 3

MILLWALL 1

Form coming into fixture

NORWICH CITY	MILLWALL
LWWW	LWDW

Green

Holt — Fleming — Mackay — Drury

Henderson — Francis — Mulryne — McVeigh

Huckerby — Crouch

Peeters — Sweeney

Livermore — Cahill — Roberts — Ifill

Ryan — Ward — P. Robinson — Muscat

Warner

Briggs	Lawrence
Roberts	Braniff
Jarvis	Fofana
Crichton	Gueret
Rivers	Wise

Statistics

Season	Fixture		Fixture	Season
103	4	Shots On Target	10	90
84	1	Shots Off Target	3	69
1	0	Hit Woodwork	0	2
54	5	Caught Offside	5	65
103	4	Corners	4	87
229	12	Fouls	10	294

Teenager Ian Henderson bagged a first-half brace as Norwich chalked up their eighth successive home league win of the season.

Paul McVeigh had set the victory wheels in motion with a sweetly struck 12th-minute opener, and although Darren Ward reduced the arrears in injury time, his effort was scant consolation for The Lions.

Millwall went close in the fifth minute, as Peter Sweeney's stinging first-time shot was parried by keeper Robert Green and cleared by Malky Mackay.

But it was Norwich who made the breakthrough with their first effort on goal after 12 minutes, Dave Livermore clearing Phil Mulryne's free kick only as far as McVeigh, who struck a left-foot effort that dipped beyond Tony Warner's reach.

Millwall nearly hit back immediately when Paul Ifill's powerful shot-on-the-turn was pushed away by Green. But seconds later Norwich were 2-0 ahead, as Darren Huckerby sprinted past Robbie Ryan and picked out Henderson at the far post with a pinpoint cross which the 18-year-old headed past Warner.

The Lions responded with a Tim Cahill header which flashed inches wide after the impressive Sweeney had created the opening.

Millwall's cause was not helped on 19 minutes, when Paul Robinson fell awkwardly after challenging Huckerby and was stretchered off to be replaced by Matt Lawrence.

Kevin Braniff gets a shot in.

Event Line		
12	🏆 ⊙	McVeigh (Indirect Free Kick)
15	🏆 ⊙	Henderson (Open Play)
21	🏆 ⇄	Robinson P (Off) Lawrence (On)
30	🏆 ⊙	Henderson (Open Play)
39	🏆 ▢	Ifill (Foul)
HALF-TIME 3-0		
46	🏆 ⇄	Peeters (Off) Braniff (On)
59	🏆 ⇄	Livermore (Off) Fofana (On)
72	🏆 ⇄	Mulryne (Off) Briggs (On)
79	🏆 ⇄	Crouch (Off) Roberts (On)
82	🏆 ⇄	Huckerby (Off) Jarvis (On)
90	🏆 ⊙	Ward (Corner)
FULL-TIME 3-1		

Peter Sweeney holds off Paul McVeigh's challenge.

Huckerby, who tormented the visiting defence throughout, came close to adding a third goal on 25 minutes with a shot that curled inches wide of the right-hand post, while Bob Peeters should have done better when he chested down a Sweeney cross and smashed a shot straight at Green.

Then came City's third, as Huckerby jinked past Kevin Muscat and despatched another inch-perfect pass, which Henderson fired home with a rasping angled volley.

To their credit, Millwall refused to throw in the towel, and after the break rolled their sleeves up and had a real go at The Canaries.

Kevin Braniff replaced the ineffective Peeters, and within five minutes the 20-year-old had tested Green with a long-range effort. He tried his luck again in the 65th minute, curling a fine 20-yard shot that the keeper was again equal to.

Warner then denied Damien Francis a fourth for Norwich with a smart stop from the midfielder's piledriver.

With Abou Fofana on for Livermore, Millwall went all out to try and salvage something from the game. Sweeney's point-blank effort was blocked, Braniff saw a header and then a shot both comfortably held by Green, and Mackay was lucky that referee Mark Clattenburg failed to spot him raising his arm to Sweeney in the dying minutes.

Despite bossing proceedings for long spells of the second half, it took until deep into injury time for The Lions to grab a long overdue goal, as Braniff flicked on Sweeney's corner and Ward stabbed home from three yards with virtually the last kick of the match.

League Table	P	W	D	L	F	A	Pts
9 Preston	18	8	3	7	26	21	27
10 Reading	17	8	3	6	24	19	27
11 Millwall	**18**	**7**	**6**	**5**	**22**	**19**	**27**
12 Nottm Forest	18	7	4	7	30	24	25
13 Crewe	18	7	3	8	18	23	24

❞ Dennis Wise

At half-time I said to the players, 'Look chaps, do you want to pack it in or try and get something?' And fair play to them, they rolled their sleeves up.

❞

❞ Matt Lawrence

We did well in the second half against basically Premiership players, in Darren Huckerby and Peter Crouch. It is a terrible shame for Paul Robinson - but football is like that.

❞

READING 1

MILLWALL 0

Form coming into fixture	
READING	MILLWALL
LWLW	WDWL

Hahnemann

Murty   Newman   Ingimarsson   Shorey

Hughes   Harper   Sidwell   Salako

Goater   Forster

Ifill   Braniff

Fofana   Livermore   Cahill   Sweeney

Ryan   Ward   Lawrence   Muscat

Warner

Savage	Roberts
Henderson	Elliott
Watson	Gueret
Young	Nethercott
Mackie	Wise

Statistics

Season	Fixture		Fixture	Season
102	5	Shots On Target	5	95
102	4	Shots Off Target	3	72
3	0	Hit Woodwork	0	2
58	2	Caught Offside	6	71
119	4	Corners	8	95
225	11	Fouls	15	309

John Salako struck the only goal as Millwall's promotion Play-off hopes suffered a setback at the Madejski Stadium.

Dennis Wise was down to the bare bones selection-wise in his first official game as player/manager and was forced to count his walking wounded before finalising The Lions' starting line-up.

With just one fit senior forward to call on, Wisey switched Paul Ifill to a central striking role, with Kevin Braniff tucked just behind.

But Iffs' first real impact was not what he or his team-mates would have wanted, as he hit Nicky Shorey with a clumsy challenge just inside the penalty area after seven minutes. Referee Mark Jones had no hesitation in pointing to the spot, but thankfully Tony Warner was equal to Andy Hughes's spot kick.

Millwall could have taken the lead just seconds later, but Ifill's left-foot volley sailed high and wide of the target.

The Royals then twice tested the visiting goal, as Steve Sidwell's low drive was comfortably held by Warner and Shorey's fierce effort dipped a good couple of feet wide.

Steve Coppell's side were not to be denied, however, and they made the breakthrough on 23 minutes when Sidwell broke down the right and picked out Salako, whose low shot took a deflection off Kevin Muscat to leave Warner stranded.

Instead of taking the game by the scruff of the neck, Reading

Darren Ward puts Marcus Hahnemann under pressure.

Dennis Wise shouts his instructions from the bench.

Event Line

19			Hahnemann (Dissent)
23		⚽	Salako (Open Play)
31			Fofana (Foul)

HALF-TIME 1-0

59			Muscat (Foul)
60			Braniff (Off) Roberts (On)
74			Goater (Off) Savage (On)
75			Fofana (Off) Elliott (On)
79			Salako (Off) Henderson (On)
81			Harper (Off) Watson (On)
85			Livermore (Foul)
90			Henderson (Foul)

FULL-TIME 1-0

League Table	P	W	D	L	F	A	Pts
9 Cardiff	17	7	6	4	30	17	27
10 Preston	18	8	3	7	26	21	27
11 Millwall	19	7	6	6	22	20	27
12 Nottm Forest	18	7	4	7	30	24	25
13 Crewe	18	7	3	8	18	23	24

then inexplicably took their foot off the gas and let The Lions edge their way back into contention.

With the exception of a long-range effort from Sidwell and a Shaun Goater header which flashed wide, the home team had little to offer as an attacking force.

Instead it was Millwall who piled forward and created the chances, the best of which fell to Ifill on 38 minutes. The lively frontman sprinted forward, nipping between Ivar Ingimarsson and keeper Marcus Hahnemann, only to slip as he was shaping to shoot with the goal at his mercy.

Iffs had another chance three minutes later, as he collected from the busy Tim Cahill and spun past Ricky Newman, but he dragged his shot wide from barely eight yards.

It proved to be a frustrating afternoon, compounded by the inconsistency of referee Jones, who waved away appeals for a penalty when Cahill was wrestled to the ground after 55 minutes, and then failed to spot Sidwell raising his hand to flatten Peter Sweeney.

The Lions finished strongly, but shot after shot was blocked, parried or hacked clear, as Reading's defence dug deep and held on for their sixth win in eight games.

❝ Marvin Elliott

It was nice to get called up, and then to get on the pitch too. Basically, I came on when we were 1-0 down and was put on to try and hold the ball up and get a goal.
❞

❝ Dennis Wise

They know that I haven't had the chance to pick from a fully fit squad, and those that go out there are doing everything that they can to help me out.
❞

MILLWALL 0

DERBY COUNTY 0

Warner

Muscat Lawrence Ward Ryan

Sweeney Roberts Cahill Livermore

Ifill Peeters

Morris Bradbury

Holmes Huddlestone Taylor Valakari

Kennedy Johnson Mawene Jackson

Grant

Fofana	Boertien
Braniff	Bolder
Gueret	Tudgay
Nethercott	Camp
Wise	Mills

Abou Fofana rides a challenge.

Millwall suffered an afternoon of utter frustration as they failed to break through a resilient Rams rearguard. But it took a five-star display from keeper Lee Grant to secure Derby a share of the spoils.

Time and time again 20-year-old Grant proved an unbeatable last line of defence, producing a string of stunning saves to leave The Lions exasperated.

Boss Dennis Wise should have realised early on that it was going to be one of those afternoons when striker Bob Peeters hobbled off injured after just six minutes, to be replaced by Abou Fofana.

And the omens weren't looking good when Grant produced the first of many match-winning saves to deny Tim Cahill's exquisite flicked effort on the quarter hour.

Grant was at it again after 32 minutes, when he comfortably claimed Paul Ifill's 20-yard grubber, before parrying Peter Sweeney's curling left-foot effort clear as The Lions kicked into action.

The visiting goal increasingly led a charmed life, and it took the crucial intervention of Youl Mawene just before the break to keep the scores level, as he threw himself across goal to acrobatically head Dave Livermore's effort off the line. The ball bounced up, and there was Cahill to make contact with both leather and the back of Darren Ward's head in an attempt to steer it home, nearly knocking himself out in the process.

Statistics

Season	Fixture		Fixture	Season
107	12	Shots On Target	2	115
74	2	Shots Off Target	0	97
4	2	Hit Woodwork	0	2
75	4	Caught Offside	5	70
105	10	Corners	2	98
321	12	Fouls	9	283

Tim Cahill tries to force the ball past the Derby defence.

It was one-way traffic after the break, with the Derby goal under siege for long spells and The Rams offering absolutely nothing as an attacking force themselves.

Cahill dragged a shot wide, Iffs was again thwarted by Grant, and when Fofana was flattened by a wall of three Derby players as he prepared to pull the trigger, referee Paul Danson inexplicably waved away an obvious free kick.

Aussie ace Cahill really deserved a goal for his tireless, unselfish running throughout the match, and he thought he'd got it when he met Sweeney's pinpoint free-kick on 69 minutes. But there was the keeper to block on the line once again.

It was then Ifill's turn to look on in despair as his shot was brilliantly parried, and Grant produced his best save of the lot from the resulting corner, somehow tipping Cahill's downward header over the bar to compound Millwall's misery.

❝ Dennis Wise

If we'd have stayed out there all day we wouldn't have scored. Their keeper was outstanding.

❞

Event Line		
6		Peeters (Off) Fofana (On)
45		Cahill (Foul)
HALF-TIME 0-0		
46		Holmes (Off) Boertien (On)
64		Valakari (Off) Bolder (On)
90		Cahill (Off) Braniff (On)
90		Bradbury (Off) Tudgay (On)
FULL-TIME 0-0		

League Table	P	W	D	L	F	A	Pts
9 West Ham	18	7	8	3	22	15	29
10 Preston	19	8	4	7	26	21	28
11 Millwall	**20**	**7**	**7**	**6**	**22**	**20**	**28**
12 Crewe	19	8	3	8	21	23	27
13 Nottm Forest	19	7	5	7	32	26	26

BRADFORD CITY 3

MILLWALL 2

Bryan Robson's reign at Bradford got off to a winning start, as a last-gasp goal ended their 12-match winless run.

Substitute Michael Branch beat the offside trap and lifted the ball over Tony Warner to cap an amazing recovery.

Tim Cahill and on-loan Everton striker Nick Chadwick put the Lions 2-0 up at the break, but Bradford stormed back, as substitute Danny Cadamarteri pulled one back and Andy Gray equalised.

It was City's first win in the League since mid-September and couldn't have been secured in more dramatic fashion.

Millwall suffered a blow in the 12th minute when Robbie Ryan was forced off through injury, to be replaced by Stuart Nethercott.

The Lions were soon celebrating, however. Abou Fofana's cross found Chadwick with the goal at his mercy, but goalkeeper Alan Combe pulled off a stunning block. The ball came out to Cahill, who slotted home his first goal in two months.

Form coming into fixture

BRADFORD CITY	MILLWALL
LDDL	WLLD

Combe

Francis Gavin Atherton Heckingbottom

Summerbee Kearney Farrelly Muirhead

Windass Gray

Chadwick

Cahill

Fofana Livermore Roberts Sweeney

Ryan Lawrence Ward Muscat

Warner

Cadamarteri Nethercott
Branch Braniff
Davies Wise
Bower Gueret
Emanuel Elliott

Statistics

Season	Fixture		Fixture	Season
93	8	Shots On Target	7	114
100	4	Shots Off Target	3	77
1	0	Hit Woodwork	0	4
70	3	Caught Offside	6	81
101	5	Corners	3	108
263	11	Fouls	14	335

Tim Cahill opens the scoring.

Abou Fofana nips past a Bradford defender.

Event Line

12	⚽ ⮂	Ryan (Off) Nethercott (On)
19	⚽ ⊙	Cahill (Open Play)
22	⚽ ☐	Francis (Foul)
24	⚽ ⊙	Chadwick (Open Play)

HALF-TIME 0-2

46	⚽ ⮂	Muirhead (Off) Cadamarteri (On)
52	⚽ ⊙	Cadamarteri (Open Play)
69	⚽ ⊙	Gray (Open Play)
74	⚽ ⮂	Roberts (Off) Braniff (On)
78	⚽ ⮂	Cadamarteri (Off) Branch (On)
78	⚽ ☐	Fofana (Foul)
89	⚽ ⮂	Cahill (Off) Wise (On)
90	⚽ ⊙	Branch (Open Play)

FULL-TIME 3-2

League Table	P	W	D	L	F	A	Pts
9 Cardiff	20	8	7	5	34	21	31
10 Preston	20	8	4	8	26	23	28
11 Millwall	**21**	**7**	**7**	**7**	**24**	**23**	**28**
12 Crewe	20	8	3	9	21	24	27
13 Nottm Forest	20	7	5	8	32	29	26

After Bradford debutant Gareth Farrelly was denied by Warner, The Lions doubled their advantage in the 25th minute. Neat interplay found Chadwick on the edge of the box and he unleashed a stunning strike which flew into the top corner.

Chadwick tried his luck again on the half-hour, but Combe came out on top, just as he did when faced with a fierce Fofana volley.

Bradford were the first to go close in the second half when Nicky Summerbee played a clever ball to Gray, whose low cross was turned just wide by Dean Windass.

But The Bantams managed to convert a minute later, as Cadamarteri latched onto a long ball into the box, cut inside and drilled a low shot which was too powerful for Warner.

Chadwick then went close for The Lions, just failing to make full contact with a header, after Bradford had failed to clear their lines.

Gray stabbed an effort over in the 62nd minute, and it was the Scot who deservedly drew Bradford level seven minutes later.

Paul Heckingbottom slid in to win back possession after some slack play from Millwall, the ball broke to Gray, and he advanced into the box and found the net with a low left-foot shot.

Windass was allowed a free header off Summerbee's quickly-taken set-piece with two minutes left, but his effort lacked power and was straight at Warner.

Then came Branch's assured finish to earn Bradford only their second home win of the season.

❝ Dennis Wise

This was a game we clearly should have won. At 2-0 up we were comfortable, having played well in the first half. But in the second, we simply didn't defend. They put us under a bit of pressure, not a massive amount, and we caved in. Quite what Muzzy was doing for the first goal, I don't know. Then Peter Sweeney gifted them the second, and for some reason we tried to play offside for the third. I don't ask them to play offside, I simply ask them to defend.

❞

MILLWALL · 0

NORWICH CITY · 0

Form coming into fixture
MILLWALL	NORWICH CITY
LLDL	LDDW

Warner

Muscat · Lawrence · Ward · Livermore

Sweeney · Roberts · Cahill · Fofana

Chadwick

Peeters

Crouch · Huckerby

McVeigh · Holt · Mulryne · Henderson

Drury · Mackay · Fleming · Edworthy

Green

Braniff	Brennan
Nethercott	Jarvis
Gueret	Crichton
Wise	Francis
Elliott	Roberts

Ten-man Millwall battled superbly to secure a share of the spoils, but the game was marred by Darren Huckerby's theatrics.

Lions skipper Kevin Muscat was dismissed for a second bookable offence on 79 minutes, but he appeared to be the victim of some over-exaggeration from the Norwich player, who rolled around clutching both of his shins in apparent agony after an innocuous-looking clash between the two.

Unlike Huckerby, who was lucky to escape punishment of any sort from referee Mike Thorpe, team-mate Paul McVeigh was rightly booked for diving after 12 minutes.

City's play-acting left an unsavoury taste at the end of what was another encouraging afternoon's work from the depleted Lions.

Despite missing 11 players, and then losing striker Bob Peeters to a calf strain at half-time, Millwall showed more composure and quality whilst in possession than The Canaries, who rarely performed to the level one would expect of a team sitting second in the table.

There were just 29 seconds on the clock when Abou Fofana caused panic in the visiting defence, curling in a cross just inches away from Nick Chadwick's right boot.

Bob Peeters holds off Craig Fleming.

Statistics

Season	Fixture		Fixture	Season
122	8	Shots On Target	4	134
81	4	Shots Off Target	4	118
4	0	Hit Woodwork	0	1
83	2	Caught Offside	6	81
111	3	Corners	1	131
348	13	Fouls	12	294

Darren Ward goes up for a header with Peter Crouch.

League Table	P	W	D	L	F	A	Pts
9 Sunderland	21	9	7	5	24	17	34
10 Preston	21	9	4	8	30	24	31
11 Millwall	22	7	8	7	24	23	29
12 Nottm Forest	22	7	7	8	34	31	28
13 Crewe	21	8	4	9	22	25	28

Andy Roberts' 18-yarder was then deflected clear, while Tim Cahill saw his drilled effort brilliantly parried by keeper Robert Green. Chadwick, making his home debut for The Lions, came close to breaking the deadlock after 30 minutes, only for his bullet header to be cleared by Green, who then somehow kept out the follow-up.

Norwich's best chance of the half came on 21 minutes, when Huckerby's effort was parried by Tony Warner and Darren Ward cleared with a timely header off the line.

Millwall introduced Kevin Braniff for Peeters at the start of the second half, and five minutes later he set up Peter Sweeney with a neat pass, but the Scottish U21 international thumped his shot straight at Green from 20 yards.

Seconds later, Fofana set off on a superb solo run and worked his way into a good position, but he dragged his shot wide of the post.

Millwall continued to look the more likely to score, and even when handed a man-advantage following Muscat's dismissal, City were unable to pose any problems for a resilient Lions' back four.

And the visitors were let off the hook deep into injury time, as Chadwick burst clear of a static defence and had the goal at his mercy, but he drove the ball straight at Green, who couldn't believe his luck.

❝ Dennis Wise

I've just taken two press men to watch the video because one of them said that Kevin Muscat stamped on Darren Huckerby. And, no, he didn't.

❞

❝ Andy Roberts

We were pleased with the way we played. We looked solid at the back and good going forward at times, but we just couldn't stick the ball in the back of the net.

❞

Fixture Type: **Division One**

Date: **Sat, 13th December 2003**

Venue: **The Den**

Attendance: **9,829**

Referee: **I.Williamson**

MILLWALL 0

IPSWICH TOWN 0

Form coming into fixture

MILLWALL	IPSWICH TOWN
LDLD	WWDW

Line-up:

Warner

Muscat   Lawrence   Ward   Livermore

Sweeney   Roberts   Cahill   Fofana

Chadwick   Braniff

Kuqi   D.Bent

Westlake   Magilton   Bart-Williams   Wright

Richards   Santos   McGreal   Wilnis

Davis

Wise	Mahon
Quigley	Counago
Gueret	Reuser
Nethercott	Price
Elliott	Bowditch

Millwall's goal drought continued as Dennis Wise's men drew a blank for the third successive match at The Den.

The Lions simply couldn't find a way through a packed Ipswich rearguard, despite having a man-advantage following the 51st-minute dismissal of George Santos for a second bookable offence.

The game itself proved to be a fairly scrappy encounter, with both teams struggling to maintain any real fluidity.

Ipswich started the stronger and should have been a goal ahead after just 13 seconds, when Cahill's poor headed clearance fell to Darren Bent, but the young striker drilled the ball wide of the target.

Town continued to enjoy more possession in the early stages and could have broken the deadlock on eight minutes had defender John McGreal made better contact with Jim Magilton's free kick.

Millwall suffered another injury blow when Abou Fofana became the 12th casualty on the club's horrendous injury list, limping off after 18 minutes to be replaced by player/manager Wise.

However, with Sweeney switching to the left flank, The Lions

Nick Chadwick heads clear.

Statistics

Season	Fixture		Fixture	Season
124	2	Shots On Target	0	159
88	7	Shots Off Target	5	129
5	1	Hit Woodwork	0	4
85	2	Caught Offside	6	91
115	4	Corners	1	150
359	11	Fouls	17	275

Tim Cahill outfoxes Matt Richards.

	Event Line	
7		Santos (Foul)
8		Livermore (Foul)
18		Fofana (Off) Wise (On)
33		Richards (Foul)
	HALF-TIME 0-0	
46		Kuqi (Off) Counago (On)
46		Westlake (Off) Mahon (On)
51		Santos (Foul)
52		Magilton (Dissent)
67		Sweeney (Foul)
78		Cahill (Foul)
82		Warner (Ung Conduct)
84		Mahon (Off) Reuser (On)
88		Braniff (Off) Quigley (On)
	FULL-TIME 0-0	

created their first chance of the afternoon, courtesy of a spectacular Kevin Braniff overhead kick, which Kelvin Davis was equal to.

The home side had a real let-off on 24 minutes. Shefki Kuqi looked odds-on to score when Tony Warner pushed Fabian Wilnis' deflected cross invitingly into his path six yards out, but he fired wide.

That scare finally stirred Wise's side into action, and within seconds Sweeney, who started well but faded as the game wore on, saw a superb curling effort from the left smack the inside of the post.

Nick Chadwick went equally close three minutes before the break, firing Braniff's cross onto the top of the bar from close range.

Millwall finished the half in control, with Braniff's 18-yard right-foot rocket flashing inches wide after McGreal had only half-cleared Kevin Muscat's free kick.

Lady luck seemed to be shining on The Lions five minutes after the restart when Santos, previously booked in the seventh minute for a foul on Sweeney, was dismissed for obstructing Braniff.

Millwall kept up the pressure as they strove to break the resolve of Town's remaining 10 men. Cahill drove wide and Chadwick headed off target, but for all their possession, The Lions were let down by the quality of deliveries into the danger zone.

With a last-ditch roll of the dice to break the deadlock, Wise threw 18-year-old Mark Quigley into the action for the final couple of minutes – and the move nearly paid off in spectacular fashion.

There were just seconds remaining when Wise floated a free kick to Quigs, whose shot was destined for the back of the net until Wilnis got a foot in to block the ball on the line.

League Table	P	W	D	L	F	A	Pts
10 Sunderland	23	9	8	6	27	21	35
11 Crewe	23	9	5	9	27	28	32
12 Millwall	23	7	9	7	24	23	30
13 Walsall	23	8	6	9	25	25	30
14 Coventry	23	6	11	6	29	30	29

❝ Mark Quigley

I did think that for a split second I'd scored the winner. It was a good ball in from Dennis, and I had a feeling it was going to drop to me because I'd seen Wardy and Nick Chadwick challenging the keeper. When it came to me it was under my feet a little bit, but I struck it cleanly and unfortunately the defender blocked it. Probably if I'd have shanked it towards the corner it might have gone in. ❞

CARDIFF CITY   1

MILLWALL   3

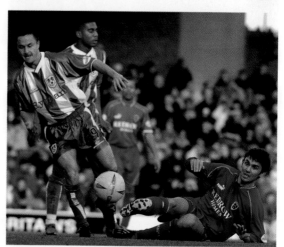

Dennis Wise takes charge in midfield.

Form coming into fixture

CARDIFF CITY	MILLWALL
LWDL	DLDD

Alexander

Weston   Gabbidon   Vidmar   Barker

Langley   Boland   Kavanagh   Whalley

Earnshaw   Thorne

Harris   Chadwick

Cahill

Sweeney   Wise

Elliott

Livermore   Ward   Lawrence   Roberts

Warner

Campbell	Braniff
Bonner	Dunne
Margetson	T. Robinson
Croft	Gueret
Prior	Nethercott

Statistics

Season	Fixture		Fixture	Season
161	5	Shots On Target	6	130
128	2	Shots Off Target	2	90
5	0	Hit Woodwork	0	5
74	5	Caught Offside	5	90
122	6	Corners	8	123
249	10	Fouls	18	377

Millwall served up an early Christmas treat with a cracking team display to secure all three points at Ninian Park.

Victory was no more than The Lions deserved in a game that saw Marvin Elliott make his full debut – and promptly walk off with the Nationwide League Man of the Match award – Trevor Robinson get his first ever taste of senior action, and both Andy Roberts and Peter Sweeney score their first goals of the season.

From start to finish it was a Millwall performance to savour, handing Dennis Wise his long-awaited first win since assuming the player/manager's role on a permanent basis on November 10.

Neil Harris, back in the starting line-up as skipper after a seven-game absence with an ankle injury, got a full hour under his belt before being replaced by Kevin Braniff.

It was Chopper who so nearly opened The Lions' account in the opening minute, when he picked up a neat ball from Nick Chadwick and curled a 20-yarder that keeper Neil Alexander did well to hold.

But the visitors didn't have to wait long to edge ahead courtesy of a fluke goal from Roberts, whose corner from the left eluded Alexander and dropped inside the far post.

Millwall knocked the ball about nicely and continued to hold the upper hand, but they had a wake-up call on 17 minutes, when Robert Earnshaw nipped in ahead of Matt Lawrence and saw his shot superbly turned away by Tony Warner for a corner.

Tim Cahill celebrates his goal.

Event Line

5 ⚽ Roberts (Corner)

30 👕 ⚽ Thorne (Open Play)

HALF-TIME 1-1

59 ▢ Livermore (Foul)

61 ⇄ Harris (Off) Braniff (On)

65 ⚽ Cahill (Open Play)

69 👕 ⇄ Whalley (Off) Campbell (On)

72 ▢ Ward (Foul)

81 ⇄ Livermore (Off) Dunne (On)

82 👕 ⇄ Boland (Off) Bonner (On)

84 ⚽ Sweeney (Open Play)

87 ⇄ Sweeney (Off) T Robinson (On)

90 ▢ Braniff (Ung Conduct)

FULL-TIME 1-3

League Table	P	W	D	L	F	A	Pts
9 Reading	24	11	4	9	29	29	37
10 Cardiff	24	9	8	7	41	32	35
11 Millwall	**24**	**8**	**9**	**7**	**27**	**24**	**33**
12 Coventry	24	7	11	6	30	30	32
13 Crewe	24	9	5	10	29	31	32

Wise's men failed to heed the warning, and The Bluebirds were back on level terms after 29 minutes, Richard Langley spreading the ball out wide to Rhys Weston, who in turn delivered a low cross that Peter Thorne swept home with aplomb.

Elliott and Chadwick then combined to set up Harris just before the break, only for Alexander to athletically palm away the Millwall striker's left-foot volley for a corner.

Cardiff went close to taking the lead six minutes after the restart when dangerman Earnshaw's low shot was comfortably held by Warner, but it was The Lions who went from strength to strength as the match wore on.

Their measured football tested the home defence and it was no real surprise when a second goal followed on 67 minutes, Wise dinking the ball in for the flying Tim Cahill to send a diving header beyond Alexander's grasp.

Despite losing Dave Livermore 11 minutes later with an horrendous facial injury, even better was to follow from Millwall.

There appeared to be few options when Sweeney picked up Cahill's centre, but with a deft piece of footwork the young Scot found space and thumped a precision finish into the bottom corner.

It took a fine fingertip save by Warner off Thorne to prevent Cardiff reducing the arrears immediately, whilst at the other end young Robinson, on for Sweeney, nearly marked his debut in sensational style when, with his first touch in League football, he hit a 22-yard sizzler a foot wide of the target.

❝ Dennis Wise

This is a tough place to come, and we are all delighted with the three points. We have found goals a bit hard to come by recently, but we got reward for our efforts and deserved to win.
❞

❝ Marvin Elliott

It was exciting, but also a bit nerve-wracking. I was nervous to start with, but once I had a few touches I was alright. The early goal helped us to get into our stride better and I felt a bit more relaxed.
❞

CRYSTAL PALACE 0

MILLWALL 1

Neil Harris hit his fifth goal of the season, but it was Tony Warner who stole the headlines with an outstanding individual display.

There was no doubting the immense satisfaction felt by everyone in the Lions camp at a job well done, especially taking into account that five players were suffering from food poisoning and vomited in the dressing room at half time.

In a bright opening for Millwall, Nick Chadwick sent an angled drive wide of Thomas Myhre's goal, whilst Harris tried his luck with a snap shot, following neat play from Marvin Elliott and Andy Roberts.

But Palace soon began to find their feet on a slippery Selhurst surface and started to ask questions of the Millwall defence.

It took a timely interception from the impeccable Matt Lawrence to clear the danger on eight minutes after Michael Hughes's mazy run had caught The Lions napping.

Julian Gray and Hughes then warmed the palms of Warner's hands with strong shots as The Eagles threatened to take control.

But Chopper took the sting out of the situation with a perfectly placed shot. The busy Elliott did well to shrug off a couple of Palace challenges and slip the ball to Chadwick. He in turn laid it off to Chopper, whose precision finish gave Myhre no chance.

Yet just seconds after the restart, Iain Dowie's side were handed a prime opportunity to haul themselves level, as Elliott's underhit back

Form coming into fixture

C PALACE	MILLWALL
LLWW	LDDW

Myhre

Butterfield Symons Popovic Borrowdale

Routledge Riihilahti Hughes Gray

Shipperley Johnson

Harris Chadwick

Cahill

Sweeney Wise

Elliott

Livermore Lawrence Ward Roberts

Warner

Black Braniff
Freedman Fofana
Berthelin Peeters
Fleming Gueret
Derry Nethercott

Season	Fixture		Fixture	Season
118	3	Shots On Target	1	131
124	11	Shots Off Target	1	91
9	2	Hit Woodwork	0	5
85	4	Caught Offside	3	93
143	9	Corners	0	123
305	10	Fouls	12	389

Peter Sweeney rides a challenge from Julian Gray.

Neil Harris hails his winning strike.

Event Line		
18	⊙	Harris (Open Play)
20	☐	Warner (Foul)
26	☐	Elliott (Foul)
HALF-TIME 0-1		
49	☐	Sweeney (Dissent)
60	⇄	Harris (Off) Braniff (On)
68	⇄	Sweeney (Off) Fofana (On)
75	⇄	Riihilahti (Off) Black (On)
77	⇄	Chadwick (Off) Peeters (On)
84	⇄	Borrowdale (Off) Freedman (On)
FULL-TIME 0-1		

League Table	P	W	D	L	F	A	Pts
8 West Ham	25	9	11	5	33	23	38
9 Reading	25	11	4	10	29	32	37
10 Millwall	25	9	9	7	28	24	36
11 Cardiff	25	9	8	8	41	33	35
12 Crewe	25	10	5	10	32	32	35

pass was picked up by Andy Johnson, and the striker's forward run was brought to a halt by a clumsy challenge from Warner.

If the home fans were frustrated that Denzil was only shown a yellow card, they were positively steaming when he pulled off a sensational one-handed save to claw Johnson's spot kick away.

Danny Butterfield's 20-yarder was then tipped over, and defender Kit Symons smacked the post from close range from a deep corner.

Millwall pressed and nearly grabbed a second two minutes before the break. Harris charged forward and the ball bounced clear to Dennis Wise, who controlled it before cracking a low drive which Myhre spilled. Unfortunately, the angle was too tight for either Chopper or Chadwick to smash the follow-up home.

The game adopted a similar pattern after the break, with The Lions forced onto the back foot as Palace probed, but to no avail.

Warner was at his best to clear a dangerous Gray cross, before pulling off a stupendous save to tip Neil Shipperley's header over.

Wayne Routledge clipped the top of the bar with a 65th-minute header and Johnson's cheeky overhead kick bounced inches wide as Dowie's men piled forward in a frantic finale.

How apt, then, that the final word should belong to Denzil, who somehow managed to block Johnson's injury-time shot on the line after it had smacked the foot of the post, breaking Palace's hearts one last time.

❞ Ray Wilkins

You take the good fortune when it comes your way, just as you accept it when you suffer bad luck. We did ride our luck today, but our players also put in a lot of hard work out there and given that four or five of them were suffering, that was very pleasing.

❞

❞ Tony Warner

It was an important penalty save. I think we rode our luck a little bit it was good for us and good for the fans. It's a derby game so people work with rival fans - and now we've given ours something to sing and dance about!

❞

MILLWALL 1

GILLINGHAM 2

Form coming into fixture

MILLWALL	GILLINGHAM
DDWW	WDLW

Warner

Muscat   Lawrence   Ward   Livermore

Roberts

Sweeney   Fofana

Cahill

Chadwick   Harris

Sidibe   Shaw

James   Perpetuini   Smith   Hessenthaler

Hills   Cox   Hope   Nosworthy

Vaesen

Wise   Saunders
Peeters   Spiller
Gueret   T.Johnson
Elliott   Bossu
Braniff   L.Johnson

Kevin James snatched a sensational last-gasp winner as Gillingham stretched their incredible unbeaten record against Millwall to 10 League games.

There seemed to be little danger when the fleet-footed forward collected the ball some 30 yards out, but he went for goal and curled an unstoppable shot into the top-right corner.

The loss of precious Play-off points was a sickener for Millwall, who had recovered from a poor first-half display to look more than capable of taking a point, if not all three.

Lions boss Dennis Wise made two changes from the side that had beaten Palace on Boxing Day, bringing in Abou Fofana and Kevin Muscat, while dropping himself and Marvin Elliott to the bench.

Right-back Muscat was twice involved in early Millwall moves. First, on 15 minutes, he threaded the ball through to Nick Chadwick, who hit a rasping angled drive a foot wide of the post.

Muscat's dink four minutes later caused chaos in the visiting defence, and when Darren Ward's flick-on found Neil Harris, the latter's looping header was brilliantly tipped away by Nico Vaesen.

The significance of that save became apparent just seconds later when Gills player/manager Andy Hessenthaler saw his 18-yard drive

Abou Fofana gets past Andy Hessenthaler.

Statistics

Season	Fixture		Fixture	Season
137	6	Shots On Target	6	121
98	7	Shots Off Target	2	152
5	0	Hit Woodwork	0	4
95	2	Caught Offside	5	93
131	8	Corners	3	150
399	10	Fouls	15	363

Nick Chadwick scores the equaliser.

Event Line

21   ⊙ Hessenthaler (Open Play)

40   ⮂ Perpetuini (Off) Saunders (On)

HALF-TIME 0-1

46   ⮂ Fofana (Off) Wise (On)

46   ⮂ Hessenthaler (Off) Spiller (On)

56   ⊙ Chadwick (Open Play)

65   ⮂ Sidibe (Off) T Johnson (On)

77   ⮂ Chadwick (Off) Peeters (On)

81   ☐ T Johnson (Foul)

86   ☐ Harris (Dissent)

90   ⊙ James (Open Play)

FULL-TIME 1-2

League Table	P	W	D	L	F	A	Pts
8 Preston	26	11	7	8	39	30	40
9 Reading	26	11	5	10	30	33	38
10 Millwall	26	9	9	8	29	26	36
11 Crewe	26	10	6	10	32	32	36
12 Cardiff	26	9	8	9	42	35	35

take a wicked deflection to put the visitors ahead.

Gillingham clearly had the bit between their teeth, and with the half drawing to a close, it took the athleticism of keeper Tony Warner to prevent them adding to their tally, as he saved supremely from John Hills and former Lions' striker Paul Shaw.

Having watched in frustration from the sidelines during the opening 45 minutes, Wise decided to try and influence matters by introducing himself to the fray at the expense of Fofana.

His impact was immediate, as he combined with Harris to set up Tim Cahill, only for the midfielder to lash a shot into the side netting.

Harris then did likewise and Chadwick twice hit efforts straight at Vaesen from good positions.

But it proved to be third time lucky for the on-loan striker when he finally got the goal he and The Lions deserved, thumping home from close range after Vaesen had parried Cahill's 56th-minute effort.

Gillingham responded by introducing Tommy Johnson, and the former Celtic striker could count himself lucky that his wild kick at Wise went unseen by referee Paul Armstrong.

Johnson was eventually booked for a crude challenge on Muscat after 80 minutes, by which point The Lions should have had three points safely wrapped up. Cahill was denied by a smart stop from Vaesen, and Wise fired wide of the target after the busy keeper had parried Harris's stinging shot.

And then, with the seconds ticking away, up popped James to snatch victory for Gillingham in dramatic style with his glorious strike.

❝ Ray Wilkins

I'm sure if we'd have started the first half as we started the second, we'd have won the game and won it comfortably, I'm convinced of that. We owe the crowd the commitment we put in during the second half, and we have to start better on our own patch.

❞

❝ Dennis Wise

When we came off the field many of the punters were clapping us because they had seen what a one-sided affair it had been in the second-half.

❞

MILLWALL 2

WALSALL 1

	Warner		
Muscat	Lawrence	Ward	Livermore
	Roberts		
Wise		Sweeney	
	Cahill		
Braniff		Harris	
	Birch	Leitao	
Wrack	Samways	Emblen	Osborn
Aranalde	Roper	Ritchie	Bazeley
	Walker		

Gueret   Allaway
Cogan   Carbon
Elliott   Vincent
Fofana   J. Lawrence
Quigley   Hawley

Statistics		
5	Shots On Target	6
4	Shots Off Target	3
0	Hit Woodwork	0
3	Caught Offside	2
4	Corners	4
10	Fouls	13

Kevin Braniff and Tim Cahill grabbed first-half goals as Millwall triumphed in this F.A. Cup Third Round clash against Walsall.

An ill-disciplined Walsall saw goalscorer Leitao booked for a 65th-minute off the ball challenge on Wise, and the ink had barely dried in referee Richard Beeby's book when the Walsall striker was sent off for a crude two-footed tackle on The Lions' player/manager.

There could have been few complaints in the visiting camp about that decision, and none either in injury time when goalkeeper James Walker was shown a straight red for violent conduct.

The game ended in chaos as The Saddlers finished with nine men and no keeper, having used all three subs.

It had all started so well for the Midlands outfit, who edged 1-0 ahead on 12 minutes when Livermore made a hash of clearing the danger and Leitao nipped in to lash the ball home.

It took another nine minutes for The Lions to test the Walsall rearguard, Matt Lawrence sweeping the ball forward to Braniff, who worked his way into the danger zone before despatching a cross-shot that Walker did well to hold, with Cahill charging in.

Tim Cahill celebrates in style.

Dennis Wise embraces goalscorer Kevin Braniff.

Neil Harris was twice frustrated by tight offside decisions, but his hard work finally paid off after 33 minutes, when he picked up Kevin Muscat's pass, swerved past two challenges and threaded an inch-perfect ball which Braniff calmly slotted home.

Millwall's efforts were rewarded again seconds before the break, when Cahill headed Wise's deep cross past Walker.

The second half was one-way traffic, with The Lions playing a neat passing game and enjoying the vast majority of possession.

There was, however, a timely reminder that Walsall could still cause a problem or two, and it took a fabulous tackle by Livermore on Leitao to deny the frontman as he shaped to shoot.

At the other end, the biggest mystery was how Millwall failed to add to their goal tally.

Harris saw two efforts blocked on the line, and Cahill smashed the ball straight at Walker from close range.

Harris then had a great chance to add a third Millwall goal 14 minutes from time, but he was slightly off-balance when the ball broke to him from a Wise corner and he ballooned over from three yards.

Walsall's misery was complete in the dying seconds when Walker saw red for pushing Wise in the face, after the boss had tried to placate the keeper, who had run upfield to argue with the official.

&& Dennis Wise

We want to get as far as we can in this competition and hopefully get a home tie in the next round and pack The Den out.

"

Event Line	
12 ⚽ Leitao (Open Play)	
33 ⚽ Braniff (Open Play)	
45 ⚽ Cahill (Open Play)	
45 □ Birch (Dissent)	
HALF-TIME 2-1	
58 ⇄ Samways (Off) J Lawrence (On)	
64 □ Aranalde (Ung Conduct)	
65 □ Leitao (Foul)	
70 ▨ Leitao (Foul)	
71 ⇄ Sweeney (Off) Fofana (On)	
82 □ Cahill (Foul)	
84 ⇄ Aranalde (Off) Vincent (On)	
89 ⇄ Cahill (Off) Elliott (On)	
90 ⇄ Birch (Off) Hawley (On)	
90 ■ Walker (Violent Conduct)	
FULL-TIME 2-1	

WIGAN ATHLETIC 0

MILLWALL 0

Form coming into fixture

WIGAN	MILLWALL
WWLD	DWWL

```
              Filan
    Eaden   De Vos   Breckin   Rogers

    Teale   Jarrett   Bullard   McCulloch
           Ellington   N.Roberts

           Harris      Braniff
                  Cahill
        Sweeney            Roberts
                  Wise
    Livermore   Ward   Lawrence   Muscat
                  Warner
```

Baines
Mitchell
Flynn
Walsh
Jackson

Ryan
Ifill
Elliott
Gueret
Fofana

Millwall secured a valuable awayday point with a battling goalless draw at the JJB Stadium.

While neither the Lactics nor Lions were able to break the deadlock in this match, defeat for either team would have been grossly unfair.

The two sides made up for their lack of finishing finesse with an abundance of enthusiasm, effort and pure hard graft in what proved to be one of the more entertaining of 0-0 draws.

Millwall, fielding the same side that knocked Walsall out of the FA Cup the previous weekend, did get the ball in the back of the net 12 minutes from time when Tim Cahill bundled home following an almighty scramble, but his effort was disallowed for a possible infringement on home keeper John Filan. That proved to be a huge let-off for a Wigan outfit aiming to improve on a miserable return of two wins from their previous 10 starts.

Paul Jewell's side started well enough in a game which swung from end to end throughout, and might have taken an early lead.

Dave Livermore was penalised for a clumsy challenge on Gary Teale, Nicky Eaden swung in the resulting free-kick from the right, and Jason De Vos header was pawed away by Tony Warner in the

Andy Roberts tackles Nathan Ellington

Statistics

Season	Fixture		Fixture	Season
171	4	Shots On Target	5	142
179	6	Shots Off Target	3	101
5	1	Hit Woodwork	0	5
92	1	Caught Offside	3	98
140	8	Corners	6	137
361	9	Fouls	16	415

Kevin Braniff goes up for the ball with Leighton Baines.

Event Line

5		Livermore (Foul)
26		Rogers (Ung Conduct)
26		Wise (Ung Conduct)
33		Cahill (Foul)

HALF-TIME 0-0

46		Rogers (Off) Baines (On)
53		Eaden (Off) Mitchell (On)
58		Roberts (Off) Ifill (On)
58		Sweeney (Off) Ryan (On)
70		McCulloch (Off) Flynn (On)
76		Warner (Ung Conduct)
90		Harris (Off) Elliott (On)

FULL-TIME 0-0

League Table	P	W	D	L	F	A	Pts
10 Reading	27	11	6	10	31	34	39
11 Cardiff	27	10	8	9	45	37	38
12 Millwall	27	9	10	8	29	26	37
13 Stoke	27	10	6	11	35	35	36
14 Walsall	27	9	8	10	28	29	35

visiting goal.

At the other end, Darren Ward went close with a towering header from Dennis Wise's free kick, while Kevin Braniff wasted arguably the best chance of the match, dragging his shot wide with the goal at his mercy after the Wigan defence had misjudged Kevin Muscat's long ball forward.

Then it was Wigan's turn to miss a golden opportunity, Teale slicing his shot wide of the mark after Warner had done well to parry a low shot from Nathan Ellington.

The second half saw both sides continue to attack the opposition in search of that all important, but ultimately elusive, opening goal.

Lions player/manager Wise made a tactical switch on 58 minutes, introducing fit-again duo Robbie Ryan and Paul Ifill for Peter Sweeney and Andy Roberts.

With 12 minutes remaining, the visitors looked to have stolen the victory when Cahill nudged the ball over the line after Ward, and then Neil Harris, saw efforts blocked in quick succession. But to their dismay, referee Eddie Ilderton ruled out Cahill's effort after consulting with his linesman, leaving Millwall to take one point home instead of all three.

❝ Ray Wilkins

It was quite an exciting game on a difficult pitch. Tony Warner and the lads defended well when we came under pressure near the end and we were very proud of them this afternoon. It was nice to see Robbie Ryan come on and do well against young Teale, who is a very promising player, and put in some teasing crosses. It was also good to see Paul Ifill get a good half hour.

❞

Fixture Type: Division One

Date: Sat, 17th January 2004

Venue: The Den

Attendance: 13,048

Referee: G.Cain

MILLWALL 2

SUNDERLAND 1

Form coming into fixture

MILLWALL	SUNDERLAND
WWLD	WWWW

Warner

Muscat — Lawrence — Ward — Livermore

Roberts

Wise — Sweeney

Braniff

Dichio — Harris

Stewart — Kyle

Oster — Whitley — McAteer — Smith

McCartney — Babb — Bjorklund — Wright

Poom

Elliott	Cooper
Ifill	Ingham
Gueret	Williams
Fofana	Thirlwell
Peeters	Proctor

Statistics

Season	Fixture		Fixture	Season
147	5	Shots On Target	5	207
109	8	Shots Off Target	3	155
5	0	Hit Woodwork	0	12
101	3	Caught Offside	3	82
146	9	Corners	2	156
423	8	Fouls	15	372

Danny Dichio makes progress against his former club.

Andy Fordham paraded his World Darts Championship trophy on The Den pitch at half-time, but it was a top double from striker Danny Dichio which kept Millwall on target for a Play-Off spot.

This really was football at its best, and while both sides deserved credit for playing their part, referee George Cain was instrumental in understanding the passion of the occasion, brandishing just two yellow cards when many other officials would have filled their books.

This was a match played at full pelt by two fired-up teams, and it was loan striker Dichio who proved the difference as he fired The Lions to three vital points.

Millwall came flying out of the traps and could – indeed should – have established an unassailable lead by half time.

Dichio, who had been signed on loan from West Brom four days earlier, might have grabbed the headlines courtesy of his two-goal show, but the entire Lions side deserved credit for their enthusiastic, attacking display.

Millwall made their attacking intentions clear straight from the off, as Dichio dragged an effort narrowly wide of Mart Poom's goal.

Indeed, the former QPR and Sunderland man could have had a double hat-trick inside the first 20 minutes, twice steering efforts wide from Peter Sweeney deliveries, stooping to head Dennis Wise's corner over and twice being denied by Poom's athleticism.

Neil Harris was clear on goal in the 27th minute, but he almost

Event Line	
30 ⚽ 🔴	Stewart (Open Play)
39 🔴 ⚽	Dichio (Open Play)
HALF-TIME 1-1	
59 🔴 🔄	Braniff (Off) Ifill (On)
59 🔴 🔄	Roberts (Off) Elliott (On)
62 🔴 ⚽	Dichio (Open Play)
64 ⚽ ⬜	McAteer (Foul)
72 ⚽ ⬜	Whitley (Foul)
77 ⚽ 🔄	Kyle (Off) Cooper (On)
FULL-TIME 2-1	

League Table	P	W	D	L	F	A	Pts
9 Reading	28	12	6	10	32	34	42
10 Cardiff	28	11	8	9	46	37	41
11 Millwall	**28**	**10**	**10**	**8**	**31**	**27**	**40**
12 Stoke	28	11	6	11	36	35	39
13 Crewe	28	11	6	11	37	38	39

Kevin Braniff hunts the ball down.

had too much time to consider his shot, and his indecision about whether to chip, round or smack the ball past Poom enabled the Sunderland man to sprint out and block Chopper's eventual shot for the third of 12 Millwall corners.

Such was the Lions' domination that it seemed only a matter of time before they would break the deadlock, but Sunderland stunned the home fans with an opener from their first real attack of the game, Marcus Stewart sweeping home Kevin Kyle's cross on the half hour.

But their lead lasted barely 10 minutes, as The Lions came charging back courtesy of Dichio's perfectly placed header from Sweeney's pinpoint left-wing cross.

Roared on by some excellent support, Millwall then weathered an uncomfortable period early in the second half, and gradually took control once more.

The introduction of Marvin Elliott and Paul Ifill for Andy Roberts and Kevin Braniff on 58 minutes paid off handsomely just four minutes later, as the subs combined to set up Harris, whose dinked forward ball was headed home by Dichio.

Two bookings in quick succession, coupled with some increasingly fierce challenges, briefly threatened to spoil the game.

But the professionalism of referee Cain quickly calmed any potential storm, and The Lions played out the final 15 minutes with a controlled, composed display to clinch a thoroughly deserved victory.

❝ Ray Wilkins

The referee tried to keep the game flowing. He probably should have stopped it a few times, but I thought all in all he had a very good game. Standing on the sidelines, I thought the match was fantastic. It must have been terrific to play in. It was quick, there was a great tempo, good passing and I thought our lads were absolutely outstanding.
❞

❝ Danny Dichio

I'm very happy. The boys did me proud. It was my first match since the operation on 23rd December and it was touch and go whether I'd be involved. But you can't ask for more than that.
❞

CREWE ALEXANDRA 1

MILLWALL 2

Form coming into fixture

CREWE ALEX	MILLWALL
WDWL	WLDW

Ince

B.Jones Wright Foster Tonkin

Sorvel Lunt Higdon Rix

Edwards S.Jones

Braniff Dichio

Sweeney Elliott Roberts Ifill

Livermore Ward Lawrence Muscat

Marshall

J.Robinson	Fofana
Tomlinson	Sutton
Moses	Gueret
Walker	Ryan
Bell	Peeters

Statistics

Season	Fixture		Fixture	Season
141	2	Shots On Target	9	156
149	7	Shots Off Target	4	113
10	0	Hit Woodwork	0	5
101	1	Caught Offside	2	103
130	4	Corners	7	153
258	6	Fouls	20	443

Danny Dichio collected his second successive two-goal haul as Millwall fired out a timely reminder to those who had already written off The Lions' Play-Off hopes.

Loan signing Dichio, who had bagged a match-winning brace on his debut against Sunderland, scored a devastating double at Gresty Road with a goal in the last minute of either half.

Victory was just reward for a solid display by Dennis Wise's charges, who moved to within four points of a top-six spot.

Suspended player/manager Wise and Tim Cahill were forced to watch the action from the sidelines, alongside the injured Tony Warner and flu-ridden Neil Harris.

In came keeper Andy Marshall for his debut, Paul Ifill for his first start since November 22 and Marvin Elliott, making only his fourth full senior appearance for The Lions.

It took some time for either side to get into their stride, but it was Millwall who settled more quickly.

Peter Sweeney came close to breaking the deadlock on 11 minutes with a rasping drive which flew inches wide of the post.

Crewe's response was immediate, as 21-year-old Paul Edwards' volley flew a foot wide of the post with Marshall stranded.

Peter Sweeney holds off a challenge.

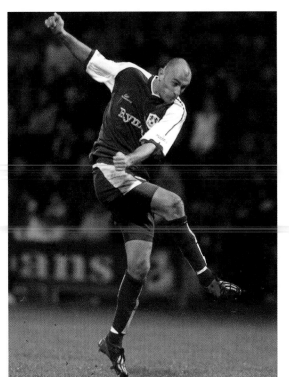

Danny Dichio lashes home the winning goal.

Event Line

44 ⚽ Dichio (Indirect Free Kick)

HALF-TIME 0-1

64 ▢ Lawrence (Foul)

65 ⚽ Roberts (Own Goal)

71 ⇄ Rix (Off) Robinson (On)

71 ⇄ Sweeney (Off) Fofana (On)

74 ⇄ Braniff (Off) Sutton (On)

90 ⚽ Dichio (Open Play)

FULL-TIME 1-2

League Table	P	W	D	L	F	A	Pts
8 Reading	29	13	6	10	35	35	45
9 Preston	28	12	7	9	43	35	43
10 Millwall	**29**	**11**	**10**	**8**	**33**	**28**	**43**
11 Cardiff	29	11	9	9	46	37	42
12 Stoke	29	12	6	11	39	37	42

But it was The Lions who forced the first save of the afternoon, Ince displaying his athleticism to pluck Kevin Braniff's shot from under the bar.

Dario Gradi's outfit then began to show flashes of the form which had reaped nine home wins thus far, as Kenny Lunt sent a 25-yard free kick over and Michael Higdon headed wide.

Millwall responded to Crewe's attack in the best possible way just seconds before the break, when Dichio latched onto a defence-splitting pass from Sweeney and slipped the ball past Clayton Ince.

Dichio nearly added a second just after the restart, only to see Ince smother his shot after Kevin Muscat had created the opening with some intelligent play.

Gradi's men hit back, and their determined spell of pressure paid off when Lunt whipped in a free-kick just past the hour mark and Andy Roberts sliced his attempted clearance beyond the outstretched hands of Marshall for Crewe's equaliser.

Wise then brought on new striker John Sutton and Abou Fofana to inject a tad more pace and purpose into Millwall's attack.

With time fast running out, Dichio dispossessed Crewe midfielder Neil Sorvel, took a couple of steps forward and then unleashed an unstoppable drive past Ince to claim a dramatic, but deserved, last-gasp winner.

❝ Dennis Wise

It was an excellent result, but not a good performance at all. We were very poor in the second half, but Danny Dichio was excellent again for us, and won us the game with a very good goal.

❞

❝ Danny Dichio

I was happy with my goals, but not my performance on an individual level.

❞

Fixture Type: **Division One**

Date: **Sat, 7th February 2004**

Venue: **The Den**

Attendance: **9,034**

Referee: **L.E.Cable**

MILLWALL 1

STOKE CITY 1

Danny Dichio scored his fifth goal in three games, but it wasn't enough to deny battling Stoke a share of the spoils.

Stoke came out showing exactly why they had taken 22 points from a possible 24, and might have been 2-0 ahead within the first four minutes.

The crowd had barely taken their seats when Carl Asaba, taking advantage of a static defence, saw his effort clip the bar and appear to bounce over the line, only for referee Lee Cable to wave play on.

The Lions breathed a sigh of relief, but they failed to heed that early warning, and just three minutes later keeper Andy Marshall was caught out of position as Clive Clarke's angled drive flashed past him and into the back of the net.

With Dennis Wise and Tim Cahill returning to midfield from suspension, it took the home side some time to find their rhythm.

Form coming into fixture

MILLWALL	STOKE CITY
LDWW	WWWW

Marshall
Muscat   Lawrence   Ward   Livermore
Roberts
Wise   Sweeney
Cahill
Dichio   Harris
Asaba   Noel-Williams
Clarke   Svard   Russell   Hoekstra
Hall   Williams   Thomas   Halls
de Goey

Ifill   Wilkinson
Elliott   Cutler
Ryan   Wilson
Gueret   Commons
Braniff   Greenacre

Statistics

Season	Fixture		Fixture	Season
161	5	Shots On Target	4	172
122	9	Shots Off Target	9	189
5	0	Hit Woodwork	1	8
103	0	Caught Offside	6	95
156	3	Corners	5	170
459	16	Fouls	12	417

Tim Cahill holds the ball up.

Danny Dichio equalises for The Lions.

The Lions' first chance came in the 11th minute, as Cahill fired over with a scissor-kick off Dichio's neat flick.

Neil Harris and Peter Sweeney combined to set up the busy Dichio on 20 minutes, but the striker directed his header wide.

But there was to be no denying Dichio, and when Sweeney sent over a delightful cross 60 seconds later, his perfectly placed header gave keeper Ed de Goey no chance.

Millwall livened up after the goal and were inches away from adding another after 40 minutes. Kevin Muscat, Harris and Sweeney created the opening, but Dichio's textbook downward header bounced a foot wide.

It took Marshall's quick reactions to deny Stoke seconds before the break, twice blocking Asaba after Muscat's weak back-pass.

Stoke's high work rate made life increasingly difficult for The Lions, who couldn't find the form and fluidity which had been so evident in the previous four games.

Marshall had to be at his acrobatic best to tip away Peter Hoekstra's free kick after 67 minutes, and Darel Russell fired wide shortly afterwards as the visitors threatened to take control.

The introduction of Paul Ifill for Andy Roberts, and then Marvin Elliott for the disappointing Sweeney, injected some pace and urgency into the home side.

The move nearly paid off when Dichio met Muscat's deep free kick, but he was thwarted once more, this time by John Halls' impeccable hooked clearance off the line.

Dichio connected with Wise's corner in the closing minutes, but his hooked volley was brilliantly tipped round the post by de Goey.

Millwall introduced Robbie Ryan in the 90th minute as a replacement for Dave Livermore, who was stretchered off with an achilles injury, and The Lions came close to nicking three points right at the death, when Ifill's last-gasp goalbound drive was blocked.

A draw was about right in the end, though the result did little to help either side close the gap on the promotion Play-Off pack.

Event Line

4	⬛ ⚽	Clarke (Indirect Free Kick)
23	👕 ⚽	Dichio (Open Play)
25	⬛ ▢	Asaba (Dissent)
HALF-TIME 1-1		
51	👕 ▢	Wise (Foul)
61	👕 ⇄	Roberts (Off) Ifill (On)
67	👕 ▢	Muscat (Foul)
84	👕 ⇄	Sweeney (Off) Elliott (On)
90	👕 ▢	Cahill (Dissent)
90	👕 ⇄	Livermore (Off) Ryan (On)
FULL-TIME 1-1		

League Table	P	W	D	L	F	A	Pts
8 Preston	29	13	7	9	46	35	46
9 Reading	30	13	6	11	36	40	45
10 Millwall	**30**	**11**	**11**	**8**	**34**	**29**	**44**
11 C Palace	31	12	8	11	45	43	44
12 Cardiff	30	11	10	9	48	39	43

❝ Ray Wilkins

We played some very good football in the first half, but our balls into the box were poor. In the second we lost our tempo, although we have to give a little bit of credit to Stoke, who made it difficult for us.

❞

Fixture Type: **FA Cup 4th Round**

Date: **Wed, 11th February 2004**

Venue: **Bucks Head Stadium**

Attendance: **5,589**

Referee: **L.Mason**

TELFORD UNITED 0

MILLWALL 2

Tim Cahill takes a shot.

Dennis Wise grabbed his first goal since the opening day of the season as Millwall shook off a resilient Telford outfit to secure their place in the FA Cup Fifth Round.

Wisey capped a virtuoso display in the best possible way, firing a blistering 20-yard effort, which gave Chris MacKenzie no chance.

The goal was no more than he deserved for a performance which inspired his side to victory against the gallant Conference team.

The Lions started as if they meant business, channelling their frustration at having made two abortive trips to Telford into a disciplined and professional performance.

Telford were on the back foot from the off, and keeper MacKenzie was tested early by Tim Cahill's ninth-minute effort.

Dave Livermore then tried his luck with a low drive which Danny Dichio deflected wide of the mark.

The lively Dichio, scorer of five goals in his previous three starts for The Lions, went close again with a deft header from a Wise cross just past the 20-minute mark.

Cahill's close-range effort was then blocked, and Neil Harris just failed to find the vital touch to a Paul Ifill cross.

Something had to give sooner or later, and the Telford defence duly did seven minutes before the break. Ifill was released by Cahill, and his powerful shot took a slight deflection on its way in.

The Lions could have doubled, or even trebled, their lead in the

Telford United line-up:

MacKenzie

Naylor Howarth Challis
Ricketts Whitehead

Hulbert Blackwood C.Moore Simpson

Murphy

Harris Dichio
Ifill
Livermore Cahill
Wise
Ryan Ward Lawrence Muscat
Gueret

Clarke   Elliott
Lavery   Roberts
Williams   Sweeney
Grant   Braniff
Rowe   McCammon

Statistics		
1	Shots On Target	8
4	Shots Off Target	6
0	Hit Woodwork	0
4	Caught Offside	1
6	Corners	8
12	Fouls	9

Dennis Wise and Danny Dichio celebrate the boss's goal.

Event Line

13 ⬦ ▢ Howarth (Foul)

37 ⬤ Ifill (Open Play)

HALF-TIME 0-1

59 ⬦ ▢ Naylor (Foul)

62 ⬤ ▢ Livermore (Foul)

64 ⬦ ⇄ Blackwood (Off) Clarke (On)

64 ⬦ ⇄ Moore C (Off) Rowe (On)

73 ⬤ ▢ Dichio (Ung Conduct)

73 ⬤ ⇄ Harris (Off) Braniff (On)

76 ⬦ ⇄ Naylor (Off) Grant (On)

77 ⬦ ▢ Simpson (Foul)

83 ⬤ Wise (Open Play)

85 ⬦ ▢ Hulbert (Foul)

FULL-TIME 0-2

minutes leading up to the break, but Telford were let off the hook as both Cahill and Dichio squandered great chances.

Not surprisingly, Mick Jones' brave battlers came out at the start of the second half with renewed vigour, and to their credit they really gave it a go to get back into the match.

But again they had good fortune on their side, as the inspirational Cahill fired over from 16 yards and Dichio sent a stinging effort narrowly wide just seconds later.

Telford refused to give up, however, and they enjoyed their best spell of the game around the hour mark. Willy Gueret, making his first senior start in over two years, worked hard against the pressure as the home side tried in vain to find a way through.

Telford boss Jones threw caution to the wind as the second period progressed, introducing three substitutes in a do-or-die attempt to salvage his side's FA Cup dream.

As Telford pushed forward in increasing numbers and with greater urgency, The Lions were able to take advantage of the gaps in their defence.

Ifill tried his luck from 30 yards with MacKenzie out of his goal, and Dichio went agonisingly close from Kevin Braniff's cross.

But it was Wise who had the final say, hitting an unstoppable shot into the bottom corner to put the seal on an accomplished team display and set up a Fifth-Round home tie against Burnley.

❝ Paul Ifill

My goal deflected off a defender. Danny Dichio said he was going to claim it, but he didn't touch it – so I'm claiming it as my fifth goal of the season. I don't think their centre half will want credit for it! We were unlucky not to score more, but the main thing is that we are through to the next round. ❞

❝ Ray Wilkins

The chairman will be pleased. Any money in the coffers is good for any club. We haven't really thought about the FA Cup but the further you get in the competition, the more you believe in yourselves. ❞

MILLWALL 1

BURNLEY 0

Marshall
Roberts
Sweeney
Braniff
McCammon

Rachubka
Chadwick
A. Moore
Orr
Weller

Danny Dichio's stunning header sent Millwall into the FA Cup Quarter Finals for the first time since 1985.

The big man's sixth goal in five games settled a bruising encounter, in which referee Howard Webb booked four players and showed Paul Weller a straight red card for flattening Dennis Wise.

Burnley had a couple of early chances, as Richard Chaplow saw his back header drop a foot wide of Willy Gueret's goal, whilst Glen Little screwed his shot embarrassingly wide following a neat build-up involving Mo Camara and Robbie Blake.

But Millwall, backed by some tremendous vocal support, began to work their way into the match, and they created an increasing number of chances themselves as the opening half wore on.

Matt Lawrence headed over after Darren Ward had flicked on a Wise corner, Neil Harris was inches away from connecting with the goal at his mercy, and Dichio headed over after a sweeping move which cut Burnley's defence to shreds.

The Lions had Gueret to thank for preventing Ian Moore from

	Statistics	
7	Shots On Target	4
3	Shots Off Target	6
0	Hit Woodwork	0
3	Caught Offside	5
5	Corners	2
15	Fouls	14

Dennis Wise celebrates the win.

Danny Dichio heads The Lions into the Quarter Finals.

firing the visitors ahead, the French keeper rushing quickly out to block the Burnley striker's effort with his legs.

Millwall finished the half strongly, with Harris' first-time shot dropping a foot over the bar and Tim Cahill sending a header wide.

The home side continued to attack after the break, with Lawrence going close following another Wise corner, and Paul Ifill smacking the bar on 57 minutes after a superb solo run.

Kevin Braniff came on for Harris just past the hour, and eight minutes later The Lions were in front. Robbie Ryan did well to keep the ball in play and square it for Dave Livermore, who switched play to Kevin Muscat on the right. Muzzy's delightful delivery found Dichio, whose powerful header gave Brian Jensen no chance.

Burnley's cause was not helped by Weller, whose red card left them a man down as the game approached the final quarter-hour.

Braniff should really have killed the tie off with a hat-trick of chances, but he scooped wide of the mark after 79 minutes and then saw his stinging effort on 83 minutes brilliantly tipped round the post by Jensen. And he had to wonder just how he managed to steer the ball wide in the final minute with only the keeper to beat.

If Bran's miss was a bad one, it was nowhere near as costly as Alan Moore's. With just seconds remaining, Ian Moore stormed down the left and delivered an inch-perfect delivery, which his namesake Alan somehow failed to connect with on the goal line.

It was a huge slice of luck for Wise's men. But there were no complaints when the final whistle went, with The Lions standing 180 minutes from the FA Cup Final.

Event Line

18	Grant (Foul)

HALF-TIME 0-0

53	Wise (Foul)
56	Wood (Foul)
61	Harris (Off) Braniff (On)
62	Blake (Off) Weller (On)
70	Dichio (Open Play)
71	Ryan (Off) Sweeney (On)
73	Weller (Violent Conduct)
75	Dichio (Foul)
77	Roche (Off) Chadwick (On)
85	McGregor (Off) A Moore (On)

FULL-TIME 1-0

❝ Dave Livermore

I don't really mind who we get in the next round. I know some of the lads fancy Manchester United, but I'd rather play them in the Final.

❞

Fixture Type: **Division One**

Date: **Sat, 21st February 2004**

Venue: **Deepdale**

Attendance: **12,903**

Referee: **K.Wright**

PRESTON NORTH END | 1

MILLWALL | 2

PRESTON NORTH END FC

Paul Ifill and Tim Cahill scored a goal in either half, as Millwall continued their push for a Play-Off place.

On the balance of play, victory was no more than the buoyant Lions deserved, and the win moved Dennis Wise's men to within two points of a top-six spot.

Preston started well, with Graham Alexander hitting a 20-yarder after just four minutes which Willy Gueret did well to hold in the Millwall goal.

But The Lions gradually began to assert themselves, and on 10 minutes Alexander had to be at his defensive best to block a dangerous Danny Dichio centre at the near post for a corner, with Cahill waiting to pounce.

Industrious midfielder Cahill was denied an opening goal just three minutes later, a dubious late flag from the linesman cancelling the volley he'd just fired home from close range.

Preston responded briefly and French stopper Gueret showed his agility to push Ricardo Fuller's piledriver away for a corner.

Whilst the first half was a fairly even affair, the balance of play shifted in Millwall's favour during the period leading up to the break.

Dichio headed narrowly wide from Sweeney's 40th-minute corner, and five minutes later The Lions were in front, with a goal that owed as much to Sweeney's persistence as Ifill's blistering pace.

There seemed to be little danger when Matt Lawrence drilled a low ball forward, but after Alexander misjudged it, Sweeney collected

Form coming into fixture

PRESTON NE	MILLWALL
WLWL	DWWD

Gould

Davis Michael Jackson Mears

Alexander   Lewis

O'Neil Keane Healy

Cresswell Fuller

Dichio

Sweeney   Ifill
Cahill
Livermore Elliott

Ryan Ward Lawrence Roberts

Gueret

Burley   Harris
Lynch   Braniff
Lonergan   Marshall
Lucketti   Wise
McCormack McCammon

Statistics

Season	Fixture		Fixture	Season
214	12	Shots On Target	7	168
194	6	Shots Off Target	4	126
8	1	Hit Woodwork	0	5
109	4	Caught Offside	3	106
196	7	Corners	8	164
413	11	Fouls	26	485

Marvin Elliott tries to beat Eddie Lewis

Event Line		
37	🔳	Livermore (Foul)
45	⚽	Ifill (Open Play)
HALF-TIME 0-1		
61	🔳	Dichio (Foul)
64	🔁	Sweeney (Off) Harris (On)
70	⚽	Davis (Open Play)
74	🔁	O'Neil (Off) Burley (On)
77	⚽	Cahill (Open Play)
80	🔁	Healy (Off) Lynch (On)
80	🔁	Ifill (Off) Braniff (On)
84	🔳	Braniff (Foul)
90	🔳	Harris (Ung Conduct)
FULL-TIME 1-2		

League Table	P	W	D	L	F	A	Pts
7 Sunderland	30	13	9	8	38	30	48
8 Reading	31	14	6	11	37	40	48
9 Millwall	31	12	11	8	36	30	47
10 C Palace	33	13	8	12	52	48	47
11 Cardiff	32	12	10	10	53	41	46

Willy Gueret barks out his orders.

and pulled back for Iffs, who steamed through the heart of the home defence to somehow get ahead of Claude Davis and stab the ball past keeper Jonathan Gould.

Preston came out for the start of the second half with an added sense of urgency, and David Healy, Eddie Lewis and Fuller all went close before their side's pressure paid off in the 70h minute, Davis slamming home the leveller from close range following an almighty goalmouth scramble.

Preston were still celebrating when Cahill was denied a second goal for the visitors by a brilliant stop from Gould.

But Preston failed to heed the warning and workaholic Tim got his just reward for another all-action display, knocking in Roberts' tantalising ball with a trademark header 13 minutes from time.

Millwall sensed that the three crucial points were there for the taking if they kept their composure, and Wise's men did just that by closing ranks and making it impossible for Preston to create any clear-cut chances.

The Lions took the win and headed back down south knowing that a victory against Rotherham United on Tuesday night could move them into a top-six spot.

❝ Dennis Wise

This is a tough place to come, but the lads played fantastic. I am chuffed about the way the players are going about their business. They are showing that they want to win things.

❞

❝ Willy Gueret

It's been a longtime to wait, but Tony Warner has done well over the last two years and so. I haven't had an opportunity to play.

❞

MILLWALL 2

ROTHERHAM UNITED 1

Form coming into fixture
MILLWALL	ROTHERHAM UTD
WWDW	DLWD

Gueret

Muscat Lawrence Ward Ryan

Wise

Ifill Livermore

Cahill

Dichio Harris

Proctor Butler

Monkhouse Garner Mullin Sedgwick

Hurst S.Barker Swailes Stockdale

Pollitt

Elliott	Baudet
Sweeney	Warne
Marshall	R.Barker
Roberts	Montgomery
Braniff	Minto

Tim Cahill delights the crowd with his late winner.

Tim Cahill grabbed a dramatic last-gasp winner as Millwall kept their promotion Play-Off dream alive with three priceless points.

Dennis Wise's men looked to have victory sewn up courtesy of Neil Harris's 37th-minute opener.

But it proved to be a real emotional rollercoaster for The Den faithful, as Michael Proctor hauled Rotherham level with a 90th-minute penalty, only for Cahill to send home an unstoppable header deep into injury time.

It was a fitting reward for another industrious display from the Aussie midfielder, who marked his 200th League appearance for The Lions with his 50th League goal.

Victory was probably no more than Millwall deserved, though the home side laboured for spells in a game which only really took off as a spectacle in those dying minutes.

Still, sometimes it's not the quality of performance, but the quantity of effort put in which proves decisive, and The Lions worked hard to dig out a crucial result.

Ronnie Moore's side settled into their stride early and went close to breaking the deadlock in the 10th minute, when Martin Butler was denied a certain goal by a timely block from Kevin Muscat.

Shaun Barker then headed Darren Garner's corner over as The Lions' defence looked surprisingly ill-at-ease during the opening exchanges. But driven on by the relentless work-rate of Cahill and Harris, the home side battled and scrapped their way back.

Paul Ifill and Dave Livermore both went close, whilst Rotherham

Statistics

Season	Fixture		Fixture	Season
173	5	Shots On Target	2	146
131	5	Shots Off Target	8	135
5	0	Hit Woodwork	0	5
109	3	Caught Offside	3	89
175	11	Corners	3	158
499	14	Fouls	11	402

Event Line		
38 ⚽ Harris (Open Play)		
42 🟨 Garner (Dissent)		
HALF-TIME 1-0		
63 🟨 Monkhouse (Dissent)		
70 🔄 Ifill (Off) Sweeney (On)		
70 🔄 Ryan (Off) Elliott (On)		
76 🔄 Garner (Off) Warne (On)		
76 🔄 Monkhouse (Off) Baudet (On)		
87 🔄 Sedgwick (Off) R Barker (On)		
90 ⚽ Proctor (Penalty)		
90 ⚽ Cahill (Indirect Free Kick)		
FULL-TIME 2-1		

League Table	P	W	D	L	F	A	Pts
4 Sheff Utd	32	15	7	10	47	38	52
5 Ipswich	32	14	8	10	60	52	50
6 Millwall	32	13	11	8	38	31	50
7 West Ham	31	12	13	6	44	31	49
8 Reading	32	14	7	11	39	42	49

Dennis Wise moves past Martin Butler.

keeper Mike Pollit did well to take the sting out of another shot by Iffs on 31 minutes.

A spell of sustained Millwall pressure paid off six minutes later, as Harris picked up Danny Dichio's flick, took one touch and lashed home his sixth goal of the season – and first of 2004. (Coincidentally, ref Peter Walton also oversaw the Boxing Day encounter against Crystal Palace when Chopper had scored his previous goal.)

Andy Monkhouse, who had made a great interception to prevent Dichio from scoring in the first half, pressed forward with a great run soon after the break, but he was dispossessed by defender Darren Ward as he prepared to pull the trigger.

Wise responded for Millwall with a rasping drive on 58 minutes which Pollitt did well to hold, whilst at the other end, Chris Sedgwick weaved his way past four players on a magnificent mazy run, only to be let down by his woeful finish across the face of goal.

And Sedgwick missed another golden opportunity after 66 minutes, when he somehow managed to scoop Paul Hurst's cross over the bar with the goal gaping.

Millwall attacked as the visitors started to run out of gas, Cahill forcing Pollitt into action with a header which was well saved, followed by a 25-yard shot which was comfortably held.

Peter Sweeney cleared the crossbar with a rising drive, and Dichio missed with an overhead kick, then headed over before The Lions went on to claim victory in a thrilling finale.

❝ Neil Harris

It was a massive goal for me. The pressure I've been under recently has been intense. I haven't been playing particularly well, and although the team has, which is the main thing, it's your own form you tend to scrutinise and look at.
❞

❝ Ray Wilkins

Have we ever won a game here at The Den by more than one goal? It appears that we can't finish teams off. It would be very pleasant one day to give someone a good hiding by two or three goals so the lads could relax and play some football
❞

MILLWALL 2

BURNLEY 0

Paul Ifill and Peter Sweeney shot Millwall to fifth in the table as Burnley slipped to their first League defeat of 2004.

It took Iffs just 13 minutes to grab his seventh goal of the campaign, clipping the ball past keeper Brian Jensen from an acute angle after picking up a delightful Sweeney through-ball.

And the lightning-quick Lion returned the favour on 52 minutes, setting up Sweeney, who smashed home a stinging shot from six yards.

Few would argue that The Lions were good value for the three points, with Burnley working hard, but finding it impossible to find a way past an inspired Andy Marshall, who produced a succession of top-class saves to thwart the visitors.

Neil Harris created a chance for the home side out of nothing after four minutes, wriggling free of his marker with a neat turn and then driving narrowly wide from 20 yards.

But it was the visitors who almost grabbed a shock lead just two minutes later, as Marshall tipped Neil Wood's shot round the post.

Marshall was called into action again after eight minutes, parrying Ian Moore's shot and then leaping athletically across his goal to tip away Bradley Orr's 20-yard effort.

Form coming into fixture	
MILLWALL	BURNLEY
WDWW	DWWD

Marshall

Muscat Lawrence Ward Ryan

Elliott Wise
Ifill Sweeney
Cahill
Harris

I.Moore
Blake

A.Moore Wood Orr Little

Camara McGregor May Roche

Jensen

McCammon Branch
Gueret Chadwick
Roberts West
Braniff Rachubka
Sutton

Kevin Muscat makes a challenge.

Statistics

Season	Fixture		Fixture	Season
179	6	Shots On Target	6	194
133	2	Shots Off Target	4	162
5	0	Hit Woodwork	0	8
111	2	Caught Offside	3	108
177	2	Corners	5	221
510	11	Fouls	9	413

Darren Ward heads away the danger.

Millwall were spurred into action, and they forged an opening goal with their first real attack of the game, courtesy of Sweeney's vision and Ifill's precision finish.

Iffs then fired a shot over the top from distance, whilst Tim Cahill was denied a certain goal by the fingers of Jensen, who somehow clawed his goalbound header over the bar for a corner.

The Lions had a lucky let-off after 29 minutes, as an almighty scramble saw both Ian and Alan Moore brilliantly blocked by Marshall, and then Glen Little denied as the ball pinged to and fro for an anxious few seconds before the danger was finally averted.

Midfielder Marvin Elliott curled a fine pass for Ifill seven minutes before the break, only for Iffs to pull the ball back too far with Harris and Cahill waiting to capitalise.

Burnley were out of the blocks quickly in the second period, and Marshall did well to parry a stinging cross-shot from Mo Camara.

A forceful run by Cahill ended in frustration when he ran into a trio of Burnley players in the area, but The Lions didn't have to wait long before doubling their tally.

Ifill's fabulous touch sold the Clarets defence short, and he sprinted down the right flank before picking out Sweeney at the far post. The young Scot did the rest, with a thumping left-foot finish.

Sweeney and Mark McCammon, a 71st-minute replacement for Ifill, then both went close as The Lions kept up the pressure.

Burnley nearly pulled one back in the final minutes through Robbie Blake, but there was to be no way past Marshall.

League Table	P	W	D	L	F	A	Pts
3 Wigan	33	15	12	6	46	32	57
4 Ipswich	33	15	8	10	62	52	53
5 Millwall	**33**	**14**	**11**	**8**	**40**	**31**	**53**
6 West Ham	32	13	13	6	45	31	52
7 Sheff Utd	33	15	7	11	48	40	52

❝ Ray Wilkins

I think this is a dizzy height for us, but I thought the scoreline flattered us a touch if I'm perfectly honest. I felt we deserved to win, but not by two clear goals. Andy Marshall had a superb game, and made five or six stunning saves, which we are grateful for. ❞

Fixture Type: **Division One**

Date: **Tuesday 2nd March 2004**

Venue: **Bramall Lane**

Attendance: **19,579**

Referee: **F.G.Stretton**

SHEFFIELD UNITED 2

MILLWALL 1

Form coming into fixture

SHEFF UTD	MILLWALL
LLWL	DWWW

Kenny

Jagielka   Page   Whitlow   Kozluk

Parkinson   Montgomery   Robinson   Tonge

Gray   A.Ward

Dichio

Cahill

Sweeney   Livermore   Elliott   Ifill

Ryan   Ward   Lawrence   Muscat

Marshall

Shaw	Harris
Rankine	McCammon
Boussatta	Gueret
Lester	Roberts
Peschisolido	Braniff

Millwall's 10-match unbeaten run came to an end, as Ashley Ward and Andy Gray clinched victory for Sheffield United in a bruising Bramall Lane encounter.

Paul Ifill reduced the arrears for the visitors with a 69th-minute drive, but despite camping in the United half for the remaining 20 minutes, The Lions couldn't find a way through for a second time.

Player/manager Dennis Wise was surprisingly missing from both the visitors' starting line-up and bench, as The Lions welcomed Danny Dichio and Dave Livermore back to the fold following suspension.

Millwall went into the game riding a five-game winning streak, while United had won just once in their seven previous outings.

Neither side managed to get a real grip on proceedings in a scrappy opening spell, but Neil Warnock's men began to assert some authority as the half wore on, with Ward teeing up loan-signing Carl Robinson after nine minutes, but the midfielder scooped his header over the bar, whilst Andy Marshall did well to hold a Ward header on the half-hour mark following good work by Phil Jagielka.

At the other end, The Lions began to ask questions of an increasingly anxious home defence. Tim Cahill headed straight at

The Lions celebrate Paul Ifill's goal.

Statistics

Season	Fixture		Fixture	Season
218	6	Shots On Target	5	184
182	4	Shots Off Target	6	139
7	0	Hit Woodwork	0	5
92	2	Caught Offside	1	112
207	6	Corners	10	187
404	12	Fouls	21	531

Robbie Ryan tackles Andy Parkinson.

Event Line		
3	🗒 ☐	Whitlow (Foul)
27	👕 ☐	Ryan (Foul)
HALF-TIME 0-0		
58	🗒 ⚽	A Ward (Open Play)
61	🗒 ☐	Kenny (Ung Conduct)
61	🗒 ☐	A Ward (Ung Conduct)
61	👕 ☐	D Ward (Ung Conduct)
62	🗒 ⚽	Gray (Indirect Free-Kick)
64	👕 ⇄	Elliott (Off) McCammon (On)
64	👕 ⇄	Sweeney (Off) Harris (On)
69	👕 ⚽	Ifill (Open Play)
71	🗒 ⇄	Parkinson (Off) Shaw (On)
74	🗒 ⇄	Robinson (Off) Rankine (On)
90	👕 ☐	Cahill (Foul)
90	👕 ☐	Dichio (Foul)
FULL-TIME 2-1		

keeper Paddy Kenny and Livers fired a 20-yarder wide of the mark.

The Blades were nearly punished for their frailties shortly afterwards. Marvin Elliott's hooked forward pass caused chaos in the area and from the resulting melee Cahill had time and space to choose his spot, but he somehow managed to scuff his shot into the grateful arms of Kenny.

Cahill, normally so composed in front of goal, was frustrated again 12 minutes after the restart, when he did all the hard work with a powerful forward run, only to hook the ball back a touch too early, enabling United to regain possession.

Unfortunately, just seconds later, a good attacking build-up from Michael Tonge and Jagielka provided an opening for Ward, who gratefully converted from close range with keeper Marshall stranded.

The celebrations had barely died down when Gray added another four minutes later, and The Lions looked to be down and out.

But a double substitution which saw Neil Harris and Mark McCammon introduced for Elliott and Peter Sweeney added some urgency and physical presence up front, and United began to look very uncomfortable as Millwall piled on the pressure.

The Lions' efforts were rewarded on 69 minutes, Dichio knocking the ball down for Ifill, who then struck a splendid drive from outside the area which gave Kenny no chance.

It was all Millwall now, with Cahill (twice), Livers and Harris all denied, whilst Matt Lawrence looked odds-on to end his agonising wait for a first senior goal before his goalbound effort took a massive deflection over the bar for yet another corner.

But as much as Wise's men huffed and puffed during nearly six minutes of injury-time, they couldn't find a way through.

League Table	P	W	D	L	F	A	Pts
5 West Ham	33	13	14	6	46	32	53
6 Ipswich	34	15	8	11	62	54	53
7 Millwall	34	14	11	9	41	33	53
8 Reading	34	15	7	12	42	45	52
9 C Palace	34	14	8	12	53	48	50

❝ Dennis Wise

I tried to make the substitution at 1-0, but obviously the linesman took so long I didn't have a chance. Then they got a second and you think 'here we go', but I slung big Mark and Neil Harris on and they did really well, both of them. We actually thought we were going to get something out of the game and I was very disappointed at the end not to. ❞

MILLWALL 0

TRANMERE ROVERS 0

Millwall would have to play it again at Prenton Park, after Tranmere Rovers keeper John Achterberg denied The Lions victory with a 76th-minute penalty save from Kevin Muscat.

Muzzy stepped up to take the spot-kick after Ryan Taylor was penalised for a shove on Tim Cahill.

After what seemed like an eternity, Muzzy opted to place his effort, and Achterberg stuck out a hand to push the ball over the bar.

The big Dutch stopper performed heroics for Brian Little's side, proving an unbeatable last line of defence as Millwall piled on the pressure in a frantic finale.

But a combination of some outstanding defensive play from the visitors and some unusually wayward Lions finishing meant that the two teams would lock horns once more for a place in the Semi-Finals.

Dennis Wise was a pivotal figure for Millwall, and he battled his way through 90 minutes, despite having his left leg heavily strapped early on, and then needing it re-strapped after another hefty challenge.

It was Wise who set up the first half-chance of the game, threading a neat ball through for Danny Dichio after four minutes, but the striker was muscled off the ball.

Marshall
Muscat Lawrence Ward Ryan
Wise
Ifill Livermore
Cahill
Dichio Harris
Hume Dadi
Mellon Jones Harrison Beresford
Roberts Connelly Taylor Goodison
Achterberg

Gueret Howarth
Roberts Linwood
Sweeney Navarro
Braniff Nicholson
McCammon Loran

	Statistics	
12	Shots On Target	3
8	Shots Off Target	3
0	Hit Woodwork	0
5	Caught Offside	4
8	Corners	3
14	Fouls	11

Kevin Muscat strikes his penalty.

Robbie Ryan fights for the ball.

Achterberg set his stall out as early as the ninth minute, athletically punching Paul Ifill's centre clear, with Dave Livermore blasting the loose ball over the bar from 16 yards.

Wise then tested Achterberg with a 16th-minute free kick which the keeper did well to hold at full stretch.

Iffs was then denied when his stinging shot was brilliantly blocked by Sean Connelly after good work by Cahill.

Livers' long-range effort was saved by Achterberg, before Ian Goodison deflected Neil Harris's goalbound effort over the bar and Achterberg somehow tipped Cahill's effort for another corner.

Little's men were rocking under the pressure, but they held firm in the face of The Lions' onslaught and finally showed some signs of life as an attacking force when Taylor and Gareth Roberts had successive shots blocked by Robbie Ryan and Muscat.

Still, it took until the 51st minute for Tranmere to force a meaningful save from Andy Marshall in the home goal, when he parried Roberts's vicious shot. Roberts then tested Marshall again with a left-foot rasper that the Lions keeper did well to tip round the post.

But it was Achterberg's day. He was like a magnet to the ball, none more so than when Cahill had a free header on 72 minutes from Matt Lawrence's through-ball, but again it was straight at "Big John".

The game became even more frenetic following the penalty, but with the fear that a mistake could prove costly, clear-cut chances were few and far between, and the challenge for Millwall to win their first ever encounter in Birkenhead beckoned.

Event Line			
45	🟨	☐	Dadi (Foul)
HALF-TIME 0-0			
60	👕	⇄	Harris (Off) Braniff (On)
79	👕	⇄	Ryan (Off) Sweeney (On)
90	🟨	⇄	Beresford (Off) Nicholson (On)
FULL-TIME 0-0			

❝ Ray Wilkins

This is the first time our lads have played in front of a full house for quite some time and it was fantastic to come out and see all these people in this fabulous stadium. The fans really got behind us, and I thank them for that. But the pressure will be on Tranmere a touch now. They do have this giant killing tradition and we'll have to break that.

❞

Fixture Type: **Division One**

Date: **Sat, 13th March 2004**

Venue: **Portman Road**

Attendance: **23,582**

Referee: **M.A.Riley**

IPSWICH TOWN $\qquad$ 1

MILLWALL $\qquad$ 3

Form coming into fixture

IPSWICH TOWN	MILLWALL
LWLL	WWWL

Davis

Wilnis Diallo Santos Richards

Miller Wright Magilton Westlake

D.Bent Kuqi

McCammon Dichio

Livermore Cahill Ifill

Elliott

Ryan Lawrence Ward Muscat

Marshall

Naylor	Harris
Reuser	Dunne
Bowditch	Gueret
Price	Roberts
Mitchell	Sweeney

Super-sub Neil Harris stepped off the bench and blasted a dream double as The Lions kept the pressure on the promotion pack with a superb victory at Portman Road.

Chopper thumped home Millwall's 30th-minute opener with his first touch of the game after coming on for Mark McCammon.

Darren Ward glanced home the second seven minutes later, before Chopper added The Lions' third on 49 minutes.

Darren Bent reduced the arrears for Ipswich, but it was to prove no more than a consolation as Millwall held firm for a magnificent win which kept Dennis Wise's men sixth in the table.

Striker McCammon was handed his first start of the season in place of Harris, but after a promising start to the match in which he linked up nicely with Danny Dichio, Big Mac was stretchered off following a sickening clash of heads with Drissa Diallo which also saw the Ipswich man forced off.

Although The Lions camp were shaken by the 24th-minute incident, it stirred them into immediate goalscoring action once the game restarted some five minutes later, as Dave Livermore swung in a

Statistics

Season	Fixture		Fixture	Season
250	7	Shots On Target	6	190
220	7	Shots Off Target	2	141
8	0	Hit Woodwork	0	5
140	1	Caught Offside	2	114
225	4	Corners	6	193
425	18	Fouls	25	556

David Livermore loses out.

Neil Harris scores his second.

Event Line

27 ⬆⬇ McCammon (Off) Harris (On)

30 ⬆⬇ Diallo (Off) Naylor (On)

30 ⚽ Harris (Indirect Free Kick)

36 ▢ Wilnis (Foul)

37 ⚽ Ward (Open Play)

HALF-TIME 0-2

46 ⬆⬇ Kuqi (Off) Bowditch (On)

46 ⬆⬇ Santos (Off) Reuser (On)

48 ⚽ Harris (Open Play)

52 ⚽ Bent D (Open Play)

56 ⬆⬇ Ifill (Off) Dunne (On)

58 ▢ Dunne (Foul)

71 ▢ Muscat (Foul)

76 ▢ Livermore (Foul)

78 ▢ Dichio (Foul)

90 ▢ Bowditch (Foul)

FULL-TIME 1-3

free-kick, Dichio flicked on and Harris hammered home past keeper Kelvin Davis for his seventh goal of the season.

Chopper was clearly determined to prove a point, and the busy frontman turned goal maker after 37 minutes with a perfectly flighted cross from the right which Ward headed home.

Ipswich retaliated with a brief flurry of penalty area activity, and Bent twice fired over the bar from good positions.

But any hopes the Tractor Boys had of a comeback were all but ended after 49 minutes. Paul Ifill played the ball forward for Harris to head goalwards, and although Davis palmed it onto the bar, the linesman correctly ruled that the ball had crossed the line.

Ipswich did get one goal back on 53 minutes, when half-time sub Dean Bowditch's low cross found Bent, who slotted home.

That sparked a sustained spell of Town pressure, but Andy Marshall denied Bowditch and Tommy Miller, Martijn Reuser flashed a 20-yard drive just wide, and an unmarked Jim Magilton headed wide from a Reuser free-kick.

After regaining control, The Lions might have added to their tally as the game entered the final stages, with Harris, Tim Cahill and Dichio all peppering efforts on the home goal.

But in the end, three goals and maximum points from a thoroughly convincing display were more than adequate reward for the lively Lions.

League Table	P	W	D	L	F	A	Pts
4 Sheff Utd	35	17	7	11	52	41	58
5 West Ham	36	14	15	7	51	34	57
6 Millwall	35	15	11	9	44	34	56
7 Sunderland	33	15	10	8	46	34	55
8 Reading	36	15	9	12	44	47	54

❝ Dennis Wise

I thought that the lads were magnificent. Obviously we were worried when Mark McCammon came off. He did get a fearful bang on the head and he was out for a while. Our physio Gerry Docherty had a look at him, and he seems to be OK. When Chopper came on as a sub he was brilliant and he couldn't wait to come and see me when he scored his goal. He certainly made his point! ❞

Fixture Type: **FA Cup Q.F. Replay**

Date: **Tues, 16th March 2004**

Venue: **Prenton Park**

Attendance: **15,510**

Referee: **U.D.Rennie**

TRANMERE ROVERS 1

MILLWALL 2

Two goals in the opening 16 minutes from Tim Cahill and Neil Harris sent Millwall into the FA Cup Semi-Finals for the first time since 1937.

Gary Jones reduced the arrears for Rovers shortly before half time, but The Lions stood firm to secure a glorious victory.

It was a shame that there could only be one winner, with both teams using every ounce of energy, determination and desire in a pulsating – and at times frenzied – Cup tie.

Millwall got off to a dream start after just 11 minutes, as Cahill chested the ball down following a Danny Dichio flick-on, took a couple of strides and drilled a low effort past keeper John Achterberg into the bottom-right corner.

Achterberg

Goodison   Taylor   Connelly   Roberts

Beresford   Harrison   Jones   Mellon

Allen   Hume

Harris   Dichio

Livermore   Cahill   Ifill

Roberts

Ryan   Lawrence   Ward   Muscat

Marshall

Howarth	Gueret
Nicholson	Dunne
Sharps	Elliott
Loran	Sweeney
Dadi	Sutton

Statistics		
8	Shots On Target	7
7	Shots Off Target	4
0	Hit Woodwork	0
0	Caught Offside	4
6	Corners	3
17	Fouls	19

Dennis Wise eyes the Semi-Finals.

Neil Harris thumps home his wonder goal.

Whilst that was a cool finish, Harris' effort five minutes later was a goal to grace any stage in the world.

Dichio was again involved, laying the ball into Chopper's path on the edge of the area. With seemingly nowhere to go, he swivelled and sent a stunning left-foot volley into the far corner.

Achterberg pulled off a superb save in the 21st minute, turning away a goalbound header from the dangerous Dichio.

On 31 minutes, Paul Ifill found room to work and cut inside, only to send his effort over the top.

But Tranmere were suddenly thrown a lifeline when Jones pulled a goal back five minutes before the break.

Iain Hume created an opening out of nothing on the right after being shadowed by Robbie Ryan and delivered a pinpoint cross onto the head of Jones, who made no mistake from inside the six-yard area.

Achterberg made another fantastic save from Dichio at the near post in the second half, following a perfect delivery from Ifill.

A shot by Tranmere defender Gareth Roberts was then deflected to safety in a good spell of Rovers pressure.

Millwall responded with a Darren Ward header from a Ryan free kick which Achterberg saved comfortably.

Eugene Dadi replaced David Beresford in the 74th minute and almost pulled Tranmere level two minutes later, his shot going narrowly wide.

The Lions were forced to mount a backs-to-the-wall rearguard action in the dying minutes, but held firm to claim the prize.

Event Line

11	⚽	Cahill (Indirect Free Kick)
16	⚽	Harris (Open Play)
38	☐	Jones (Ung Conduct)
38	☐	Muscat (Ung Conduct)
41	⚽	Jones (Open Play)

HALF TIME 1-2

49	☐	Livermore (Foul)
73	⮂	Beresford (Off) Dadi (On)
77	⮂	Ifill (Off) Elliott (On)
79	☐	Hume (Dissent)
82	⮂	Dichio (Off) Sutton (On)
89	☐	Sutton (Ung Conduct)

FULL TIME 1-2

❝ Dennis Wise

This is the most satisfying result ever for me. It is great for the players to be in this situation and while I am pleased for myself, I am more pleased for the players and the fans.

❞

Fixture Type: **Division One**

Date: **Sun, 21st March 2004**

Venue: **The Den**

Attendance: **14,055**

Referee: **J.T.Winter**

MILLWALL   4

WEST HAM UNITED   1

Form coming into fixture

MILLWALL	WEST HAM UTD
WWLW	DWLW

Marshall

Muscat Lawrence Ward Ryan

Roberts

Ifill Livermore

Cahill

Dichio Harris

Harewood Zamora

Etherington Horlock Carrick Reo-Coker

Harley Dailly Melville Repka

Bywater

🟥 Chadwick   Deane 🟥
Warner   Srnicek
Elliott   McAnuff
Wise   Cohen
Sweeney   Nowland

Statistics

Season	Fixture		Fixture	Season
195	5	Shots On Target	3	249
144	3	Shots Off Target	2	195
5	0	Hit Woodwork	1	16
117	3	Caught Offside	3	131
198	5	Corners	4	229
563	7	Fouls	11	448

The Lions celebrate.

Tim Cahill bagged a brace as Millwall mauled the hapless Hammers at The Den in a pulsating derby, which also saw the home side miss two penalties.

It proved to be a thrilling 90 minutes in which The Lions scored four goals in a League game for the first time since January 2003.

And it would have been an even bigger winning margin, but for the profligacy from the penalty spot of both Cahill and Neil Harris.

Striker Harris was the first to miss on 16 minutes, after Paul Ifill had been shoved off balance by a clumsy Matthew Etherington challenge. Although referee Jeff Winter was unsighted, linesman Mike Yerby spotted the offence and to the delight of the home fans, a penalty was awarded.

That joy quickly turned to despair, however, as Harris stepped up to strike the ball, but his effort hit keeper Stephen Bywater's leg, with the loose ball hacked clear for a corner.

West Ham were fairly ineffective as an attacking force throughout, only managing a single shot on target in the opening half, a Kevin Horlock 30-yard free kick which clipped the top of the bar.

Millwall continued to look the more disciplined and organised of

Nick Chadwick scores the fourth.

the two outfits, and they took a deserved lead after 33 minutes, when Iffs crossed from the left and Christian Dailly, stretching to clear the ball, managed to steer it past Bywater and into the bottom corner of his own net.

If the first half had been lacking in action, the first 15 minutes after the break more than made up for it, with three goals, a sending off and a penalty miss.

Nick Chadwick created Millwall's second goal with virtually his first touch of the ball, providing a delightful cross that Cahill powered past Bywater with a trademark header.

The celebrations had barely died down when West Ham were thrown a lifeline. Matt Lawrence was penalised for handball, and up stepped Marlon Harewood to smack home.

Cahill restored The Lions' two-goal advantage on 56 minutes with a sublime hooked volley from Ifill's corner, but then wasted a glorious opportunity to clinch his first senior hat-trick.

Then came the dismissal, as Harris sprinted to chase a long forward punt, clipped the ball past Bywater and was promptly flattened by the visiting keeper, who was shown a straight red card.

Cahill was handed the ball and promptly became the second Millwall player to miss from the penalty spot, blasting wildly off target.

Andy Marshall had been a spectator for long periods, but he proved his worth with a splendid low block to smother Brian Deane's angled drive after 62 minutes.

But order was restored and the rampant Lions were not to be denied a fourth, as Tomas Repka hideously misjudged a long ball, allowing loan striker Chadwick to thump home an unstoppable left-foot shot past replacement keeper Pavel Srnicek.

Event Line
34 Dailly (Own Goal)
HALF-TIME 1-0
46 Dichio (Off) Chadwick (On)
46 Cahill (Open Play)
49 Harewood (Penalty)
50 Horlock (Off) Deane (On)
56 Cahill (Corner)
60 Bywater (Foul)
62 Etherington (Off) Srnicek (On)
73 Harewood (Off) McAnuff (On)
77 Harris (Foul)
80 Chadwick (Open Play)
84 Melville (Foul)
FULL-TIME 4-1

League Table	P	W	D	L	F	A	Pts
6 West Ham	38	15	15	8	56	40	60
7 Sunderland	35	16	11	8	49	35	59
8 Millwall	**36**	**16**	**11**	**9**	**48**	**35**	**59**
9 Ipswich	38	17	8	13	71	62	59
10 Reading	38	16	9	13	47	51	57

Fixture Type: **Division One**

Date: **Wed, 24th March 2004**

Venue: **National Hockey Stadium**

Attendance: **3,037**

Referee: **M.J.Jones**

WIMBLEDON 0

MILLWALL 1

Tim Cahill's quality strike settled an otherwise scrappy affair as The Lions moved up to joint-fourth in the First Division with three more precious promotion points.

Midfielder Cahill thumped home his 11th goal of the season two minutes before the break to put Millwall in the driving seat at the National Hockey Stadium.

But The Dons, who came into the game riding a nine-game losing streak, had no intention of rolling over, and they belied their lowly position by making Dennis Wise's men battle all the way.

The Lions, beaten just once in their previous 15 matches, started brightly against the rock-bottom Dons, as Paul Ifill saw his left-foot effort well held by keeper Scott Bevan with five minutes on the clock.

Stuart Murdoch's side did their utmost to make life difficult for the visitors, and they weren't lacking in either effort or commitment as they rolled up their sleeves and got stuck in – too hard, in the case of Wayne Gray, who was booked for clattering Kevin Muscat.

Millwall's early rhythm was disrupted after 19 minutes when Dave Livermore was forced out of the action with a shin injury, to be replaced by Wise.

Form coming into fixture

WIMBLEDON	MILLWALL
LLLL	WLWW

Bevan

Oyedele Williams Hawkins Puncheon

Darlington Chorley Barton Jarrett

Herzig Gray

Harris Dichio

Cahill

Livermore Ifill

Roberts

Ryan Ward Lawrence Muscat

Marshall

Smith Wise
Mackie Chadwick
Kamara Sweeney
Martin Warner
Ntimban-Zeh Elliott

Statistics

Season	Fixture		Fixture	Season
153	3	Shots On Target	7	202
152	1	Shots Off Target	9	153
7	0	Hit Woodwork	0	5
120	2	Caught Offside	7	124
149	3	Corners	3	201
402	16	Fouls	14	577

Danny Dichio bravely goes in for a header.

Event Line

10	🛡 ▢	Gray (Foul)
19	👕 ⇄	Livermore (Off) Wise (On)
37	🛡 ⇄	Jarrett (Off) Smith (On)
43	👕 ◉	Cahill (Open Play)
	HALF-TIME 0-1	
46	🛡 ⇄	Herzig (Off) Mackie (On)
60	👕 ⇄	Ifill (Off) Chadwick (On)
67	👕 ⇄	Harris (Off) Sweeney (On)
69	🛡 ▢	Barton (Foul)
71	🛡 ⇄	Barton (Off) Kamara (On)
	FULL-TIME 0-1	

League Table	P	W	D	L	F	A	Pts
3 Sheff Utd	38	18	9	11	56	43	63
4 Sunderland	36	17	11	8	51	36	62
5 Millwall	37	17	11	9	49	35	62
6 Wigan	37	16	13	8	51	38	61
7 West Ham	38	15	15	8	56	40	60

Tim Cahill scores the winner just before half-time.

Seconds after entering the fray, the player/manager saw his side go close to scoring the opening goal, as Ifill's low grubber was blocked by Bevan's feet.

Neil Harris's 20th-minute effort curled narrowly wide, whilst Danny Dichio arguably should have done better with a tame header which Bevan collected comfortably.

But The Lions' first-half pressure finally told with a well-worked goal on 43 minutes. Muscat picked up possession on the right, sprinted forward, played a neat one-two and pulled the ball back perfectly for Cahill to sweep home in style from eight yards.

Wimbledon briefly threatened, and Andy Marshall did well to avert the danger from Warren Barton's 30-yard piledriver right on half-time. But a Dons equaliser at that stage would have been an injustice.

The Lions looked more commanding after the break and had plenty of opportunities to make the game safe. Cahill's 56th-minute volley was superbly pushed away by the increasingly busy Bevan, and Andy Roberts drilled the follow-up wide.

Cahill thought he had sewn up the points with a header from Wise's free kick six minutes from time, only for the linesman to flag him for offside.

Wimbledon caused a few anxious moments in the dying stages, notably when they forced a couple of corners deep into injury time. But The Lions defended stoutly and were in no mood to throw away their advantage.

❝ Ray Wilkins

It was another important result for us. It wasn't the best performance but at this stage and from now on it's all about results, so we have to be a little more forgiving. A second goal would clearly have made the game safe, but we just lacked that little bit of quality that was needed and consequently in the end gave ourselves one or two nervy moments. ❞

Fixture Type: **Division One**

Date: **Sat, 27th March 2004**

Venue: **Bescot Stadium**

Attendance: **6,486**

Referee: **S.G.Tomlin**

WALSALL   1

MILLWALL   1

Form coming into fixture

WALSALL	MILLWALL
DWLW	LWWW

Walker

Bazeley Emblen Roper Aranalde

Osborn Andrews Burley Merson

Bradbury Fryatt

Chadwick Dichio

Harris

Cahill Elliott

Wise

Ryan Ward Lawrence Muscat

Marshall

McSporran	Ifill
Petterson	Roberts
Carbon	Sweeney
Wright	Gueret
Taylor	Dunne

Nick Chadwick wins a header.

Statistics

Season	Fixture		Fixture	Season
173	4	Shots On Target	3	205
175	6	Shots Off Target	7	160
5	0	Hit Woodwork	0	5
124	3	Caught Offside	6	130
193	7	Corners	5	206
462	12	Fouls	15	592

Paul Ifill grabbed a last-gasp leveller as The Lions secured a share of the spoils with a battling display at Walsall.

An uncharacteristic error by Darren Ward looked to have handed The Saddlers all three points, as Keith Andrews capitalised on the defender's hesitation to fire home a 78th-minute opener.

But Colin Lee's side didn't bank on the sheer spirit and resilience of this Millwall outfit, and Iffs, a 46th-minute replacement for Neil Harris, smacked home a thoroughly deserved 88th-minute equaliser.

Up to the final quarter-hour there had been little to choose between the teams in what had been a pretty dire affair.

However, with the game effectively dying on its feet, Walsall looked to have seized control when Andrews, on loan from Wolves, arrived unmarked to meet Lee Bradbury's cross and drill a low shot past keeper Andy Marshall.

That goal sparked the game into life, and Craig Burley nearly put the match beyond Millwall's reach seconds later with a snap shot which flew narrowly wide.

But the never-say-die Lions mounted a late surge on the home goal, and with two minutes left snatched a late leveller, when Iffs smashed home an unstoppable shot after Walsall had failed to clear the danger from a corner.

A draw was just about the right result from a match that really

Paul Ifill celebrates the leveller.

only got going as a spectacle towards the end.

Lions player/manager Dennis Wise brought himself back into a Millwall side which showed three changes from the starting line-up that had destroyed West Ham two matches previously.

For much of the first half it was a story of midfield veterans Wisey and his Walsall counterpart Paul Merson trying to stamp their authority on proceedings.

But even the influence of the two former England internationals couldn't spark a game which rapidly degenerated into a stalemate.

It took 33 minutes for Millwall to carve out their first chance, as Tim Cahill blasted an 18-yard effort wide.

Walsall's only response in the half was a long-range Burley effort which drifted harmlessly over the crossbar.

In a desperate attempt to inject some creativity into the game, both sides opted to make changes at half time, with the hosts sending on new signing Jermaine McSporran in place of Matt Fryatt, and Iffs replacing Chopper.

McSporran's first action came on 57 minutes with a clumsy challenge on Wise that earned him a yellow card.

But this scrappy affair, seriously devoid of creative attacking ideas, finally came to life 12 minutes from time, as Andrews fired the home side ahead.

The Lions then began to seriously press the home defence, and when The Saddlers failed to clear an Andy Roberts corner, there was Iffs to smash an unstoppable volley through a crowd of players, securing a valuable point.

Event Line
28   Lawrence (Foul)
38   Cahill (Foul)
HALF-TIME 0-0
46   Fryatt (Off) McSporran (On)
46   Harris (Off) Ifill (On)
53   Dichio (Foul)
57   McSporran (Ung Conduct)
60   Elliott (Off) Roberts (On)
77   Chadwick (Off) Sweeney (On)
78   Andrews (Open Play)
88   Ifill (Corner)
FULL-TIME 1-1

League Table	P	W	D	L	F	A	Pts
3 Sunderland	37	18	11	8	53	37	65
4 West Ham	39	16	15	8	58	41	63
5 Millwall	38	17	12	9	50	36	63
6 Sheff Utd	39	18	9	12	57	45	63
7 Wigan	38	16	14	8	52	39	62

SUNDERLAND 0

MILLWALL 1

Tim Cahill's goal earned Millwall an FA Cup Final berth against Manchester United and a place in European football next season.

An error by Black Cats skipper George McCartney opened space for a Paul Ifill shot. Keeper Mart Poom saved, but Cahill was on hand to fire in the rebound.

Things were tense until the final whistle, although former Sunderland striker Danny Dichio almost wrapped the match up with an effort 16 minutes from time, which Poom saved brilliantly.

McCartney nearly equalised at the death when his 85th-minute shot curled agonisingly wide, and his side's misery was completed when Jason McAteer picked up a second yellow card and was sent off.

Whilst the Londoners settled more quickly, with Dennis Wise controlling things from the middle of the field, it was Sunderland who created the more promising openings in the early stages.

They almost took a seventh-minute lead when Cahill was penalised for a trip on McAteer, setting up a free kick 25 yards out. John Oster's shot curled over the wall and looked to have keeper Andy Marshall well beaten, but it struck the crossbar.

Oster might have saved a goal at the other end when he turned up inside his own penalty area on 17 minutes to hack away a Neil Harris cross after the hard-working striker had forced his way in.

McCartney's misjudgment led to The Lions' opener eight minutes

Poom

Wright   Breen   Babb   McCartney

Oster   McAteer   Thirlwell   Arca

Kyle   Smith

Harris   Dichio

Livermore   Cahill   Ifill

Wise

Ryan   Lawrence   Ward   Muscat

Marshall

Myhre	Gueret
Piper	Elliott
Thornton	Roberts
Williams	Sweeney
Stewart	Chadwick

	Statistics	
3	Shots On Target	3
9	Shots Off Target	3
1	Hit Woodwork	0
3	Caught Offside	2
7	Corners	2
15	Fouls	20

Tim Cahill celebrates his historic winning goal.

Dennis Wise takes a shot at goal.

Event Line		
15		Ifill (Ung Conduct)
26		Cahill (Open Play)
29		Ifill (Off) Sweeney (On)
37		McAteer (Ung Conduct)
39		McCartney (Foul)
42		Muscat (Off) Roberts (On)
HALF-TIME 0-1		
56		Ryan (Off) Elliott (On)
60		Wise (Foul)
61		Kyle (Off) Stewart (On)
76		Thirlwell (Foul)
77		Babb (Off) Piper (On)
86		McAteer (Foul)
90		Wright (Off) Thornton (On)
FULL-TIME 0-1		

later. The Northern Ireland international's lay-off to Phil Babb ran woefully short, allowing the lively Ifill to steal in and head for goal. Although Poom managed to beat his well-struck shot away, Cahill was on hand to hook home the rebound and spark delirious celebrations.

Ifill's afternoon was to end prematurely when he was stretchered off four minutes later, soon to be followed by tough-tackling defender Kevin Muscat, courtesy of a rough challenge from McCartney.

Sunderland passed up several good shooting opportunities in the half, although Julio Arca went reasonably close when he fired into the side netting from a tight angle in injury-time.

The Black Cats came out for the second half a more determined side. Kevin Kyle hammered a shot wide after his initial effort from a Steven Wright cross had been blocked, and then tested Marshall with a downward header.

The Lions might have killed the game off in the 74th minute, as Cahill broke down the right and crossed for Dichio, whose point-blank header was saved by Poom.

Sunderland boss Mick McCarthy threw caution to the wind in a desperate attempt to find that elusive goal, replacing defender Babb with winger Matt Piper.

McCartney had a glorious opportunity to level five minutes from time, but curled his effort inches wide.

Sunderland's day took a turn for the worse two minutes later when McAteer was dismissed for a second bookable offence, leaving Wise's men to march on to the Millennium Stadium.

" Theo Paphitis

I can't put it into words. It's unreal. Millwall in the Final of the FA Cup – and in Europe!
"

" Dennis Wise

It's fantastic. They've worked extremely hard. They are a great bunch of lads, and I'm proud of them all.
"

" Tim Cahill

It's all about having a bit of luck and being in the right place at the right time. It's something for the fans, not just us. It's a special day. You have to take it in your stride and try to appreciate it. It hasn't sunk in yet. They're (Manchester United) my heroes but we are going to get a chance against them in the Final and it's unbelievable.
"

Fixture Type: **Division One**

Date: **Wed, 7th April 2004**

Venue: **The Den**

Attendance: **9,584**

Referee: **M.Fletcher**

MILLWALL — 0

CARDIFF CITY — 0

A goalless draw against Cardiff City brought Millwall back down to earth after their FA Cup Semi-Final celebrations.

The Lions struggled to get any sort of attacking rhythm going in the first half, and a frustrating afternoon was capped off by the last-minute dismissal of Tim Cahill for a second bookable offence.

The Aussie midfielder was unlucky to fall foul of referee Mick Fletcher, whose performance was infuriatingly inconsistent. A classic example came just past the hour mark when he booked Cardiff's Gary Croft for a foul on Dave Livermore and then let the same player off with a mere talking to after a scything challenge on Neil Harris.

Dennis Wise's men worked extremely hard to get things going, but they just couldn't seem to find any fluidity in their play.

Form coming into fixture

MILLWALL	CARDIFF CITY
WWWD	LWWW

Marshall

Dunne — Lawrence — Ward — Ryan

Roberts

Cahill — Livermore

Chadwick

Dichio — Harris

Lee — Earnshaw

Parry — Whalley — Langley — Robinson

Vidmar — Collins — Gabbidon — Croft

Margetson

Elliott	Bullock
Sweeney	Campbell
Braniff	Gordon
Gueret	Alexander
McCammon	Barker

Robbie Ryan beats Richard Langley to the ball.

Statistics

Season	Fixture		Fixture	Season
208	3	Shots On Target	1	264
164	4	Shots Off Target	5	224
5	0	Hit Woodwork	0	9
131	1	Caught Offside	1	132
210	4	Corners	2	194
608	16	Fouls	11	403

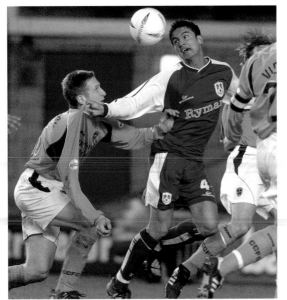
Tim Cahill gets in amongst the Cardiff defence.

	Event Line
13 ⚽ ⇄	Robinson (Off) Bullock (On)
44 ⚽ ☐	Lawrence (Foul)
	HALF TIME 0-0
46 ⚽ ⇄	Chadwick (Off) Sweeney (On)
46 ⚽ ⇄	Roberts (Off) Elliott (On)
48 ⚽ ☐	Vidmar (Foul)
62 ⚽ ☐	Croft (Foul)
71 ⚽ ☐	Lee (Foul)
72 ⚽ ☐	Ward (Ung Conduct)
74 ⚽ ☐	Cahill (Foul)
75 ⚽ ⇄	Parry (Off) Campbell (On)
79 ⚽ ☐	Bullock (Foul)
84 ⚽ ⇄	Harris (Off) Braniff (On)
84 ⚽ ⇄	Lee (Off) Gordon (On)
90 ⚽ ☐	Cahill (Foul)
	FULL TIME 0-0

The opening half was a low-key affair, with scoring chances few and far between.

Cahill carved out one of the better opportunities, his right-wing cross on 21 minutes met by Danny Dichio, whose towering header forced Martyn Margetson into a full-stretch save.

Shortly afterwards, Lee Bullock helped a long ball into the path of Wales international Robert Earnshaw, who beat Matt Lawrence, only to stab his shot wide.

Nick Chadwick flashed a 34th-minute volley just past the top corner after a neat lay-off from Dichio, while City's Paul Parry saw his fierce drive zip wide of the mark.

Wise introduced Marvin Elliott and Peter Sweeney for Andy Roberts and Chadwick at the interval, a move which added some pace and width to the home side.

Elliott was the architect of the victory against Cardiff on his full debut last December, and he twice went close to making the all-important breakthrough.

Firstly, nine minutes after the restart, the young midfielder drilled an effort that was well held by Margetson. He then thumped a 22-yard drive narrowly wide on 68 minutes after Dichio had flicked on Sweeney's free-kick.

James Collins then forced Andy Marshall into an easy save, before Elliott, Harris and Dichio all saw shots drift just wide.

Millwall were starting to take control of the match, but for all their possession, just couldn't find a way through.

They simply seemed to run out of steam in the end, content to share the spoils with the visitors.

League Table	P	W	D	L	F	A	Pts
3 Sunderland	38	19	11	8	55	38	68
4 Wigan	40	17	14	9	55	40	65
5 Millwall	**39**	**17**	**13**	**9**	**50**	**36**	**64**
6 West Ham	40	16	15	9	58	43	63
7 Sheff Utd	40	18	9	13	58	47	63

❝ Dennis Wise

It was certainly a game of two halves as far as we were concerned. In the first we looked like we were still at the party, and we didn't play well at all. At half-time we changed things and looked a lot better. He (Tim Cahill) made two tackles and got two yellow cards. He's got no complaints about the first one, but I don't know whether the second one was that bad. He's a bit gutted as you would expect. ❞

COVENTRY CITY 4

MILLWALL 0

Form coming into fixture

COVENTRY CITY	MILLWALL
WLLL	WWDD

Shearer

Whing   Konjic   Davenport   Staunton

Barrett   Deloumeaux   Gudjonsson   Warnock

Joachim   Olszar

Harris   Chadwick

Cahill

Livermore   Sweeney

Elliott

Ryan   Ward   Lawrence   Dunne

Marshall

Lowe	Roberts
Kerr	Sutton
McSheffrey	McCammon
Ward	Gueret
Doyle	Hearn

Statistics

Season	Fixture		Fixture	Season
282	8	Shots On Target	1	209
277	6	Shots Off Target	4	168
10	0	Hit Woodwork	1	6
114	1	Caught Offside	4	135
280	6	Corners	1	211
500	17	Fouls	8	616

Andy Roberts skips over a challenge.

Julian Joachim bagged a brace as Millwall slid to their heaviest League defeat of the season with a defensive horror show at Highfield Road.

The former Aston Villa and Leicester striker opened City's account on six minutes with the home side's first real attack on goal.

And it just went from bad to worse, as the weary Lions conceded further goals to Eric Deloumeaux, Joachim again and then Gary McSheffrey to slip to seventh and out of the Play-Off positions.

Millwall might have arrived at Highfield Road unbeaten in eight games, but after energy – and emotion-sapping games against Sunderland and Cardiff in the previous six days – and with player/manager Dennis Wise plus skipper Kevin Muscat out of the line-up – they were far from being on top of their game.

The Sky Blues, who had lost on their previous three outings, started brightly and were ahead after just six minutes when Bjarni Gudjonsson collected a short corner and swung the ball in to Muhamed Konjic, who knocked it back for Joachim to convert from close range.

The Lions nearly equalised three minutes later when Tim Cahill connected with Robbie Ryan's free kick, only to see his effort strike the woodwork.

Mark McCammon makes his presence felt.

League Table	P	W	D	L	F	A	Pts
5 Ipswich	41	19	8	14	78	67	65
6 West Ham	41	16	16	9	58	43	64
7 Millwall	40	17	13	10	50	40	64
8 Sheff Utd	41	18	9	14	58	50	63
9 Reading	41	18	9	14	52	54	63

Millwall were holding their heads in their hands three minutes after that, as Coventry moved into a 2-0 lead.

Again it came from a corner, Gudjonsson this time crossing for Deloumeaux to head across goal and into the net to open his goalscoring account for the club.

Graham Barrett, restored to the Sky Blues starting line-up, then fired wide before Dave Livermore did likewise for the visitors.

Barrett went close again, forcing Andy Marshall into a save with a long-range strike. Deloumeaux then had a shot blocked by Marvin Elliott.

Millwall made all their substitutions at the break, with Andy Roberts, Mark McCammon and John Sutton coming on for Ryan, Cahill and Neil Harris.

Sutton, regularly on target for the reserves since his move from Raith, could have reduced the arrears after 55 minutes, but he headed Peter Sweeney's corner into the hands of keeper Scott Shearer.

It proved a costly miss, as Coventry went down the other end and took advantage of some slack Millwall defending to notch their third, Joachim tapping home the easiest of chances for his 11th goal of the season.

If that was bad, worse was to follow when young defender Alan Dunne was carried off with a knee injury in the dying minutes following a clumsy challenge.

And to compound Millwall's misery, sub McSheffrey, a second-half replacement for Barrett, fired home a penalty three minutes from time after Matt Lawrence had been penalised for a foul on Joachim.

❝❝ Dennis Wise

We were punished for some very sloppy defending. We failed to mark properly at corners which cost us the first two goals and that is very unlike us. I can't remember the last time we conceded from set-pieces like that. The players may be tired, but that is no excuse for not marking properly in that way. 〞

Fixture Type: **Division One**

Date: **Mon, 12th April 2004**

Venue: **The Den**

Attendance: **13,304**

Referee: **S.W.Mathieson**

MILLWALL 1

WEST BROMWICH ALBION 1

Form coming into fixture

MILLWALL	WEST BROM
WDDL	WWWW

Marshall

Roberts   Lawrence   Ward   Ryan

Elliott

Wise   Livermore

Cahill

Dichio   McCammon

Facey   Horsfield

Koumas   O'Connor   Johnson

Clement   J.Chambers

Gregan   Moore   Gaardsoe

Hoult

Sweeney	Dyer
Harris	Dobie
Gueret	Kinsella
Hearn	Murphy
Chadwick	Hughes

Danny Dichio ended his 12-game goal drought, but it wasn't enough to secure victory against a West Brom side that finished the match with nine men.

Gary Megson's Baggies were already chasing the game, courtesy of Dichio's 19th-minute opener, when Jason Koumas was sent off for his second foul on Dennis Wise after 43 minutes.

But the visitors dragged themselves level 10 minutes after the break, as Andy Johnson stabbed home from close range.

The Lions looked set to claim a dramatic injury-time winner when referee Scott Mathieson dismissed Thomas Gaardsoe for a foul on Dichio and appeared to point to the penalty spot.

But after a three-minute delay, he opted to place the ball barely six inches outside the area, and the free-kick came to nothing.

A draw was just about right on the balance of play, with neither team deserving to lose, but probably not doing enough to warrant walking away with all three points either.

Millwall took a while to settle, but broke the deadlock with virtually their first attempt on goal.

Wise floated in a free-kick from the left which Dichio headed powerfully past keeper Russell Hoult.

West Brom, who came into the game looking for their seventh

Statistics

Season	Fixture		Fixture	Season
212	3	Shots On Target	3	256
171	3	Shots Off Target	2	226
6	0	Hit Woodwork	1	5
137	2	Caught Offside	1	145
215	4	Corners	6	239
635	19	Fouls	16	501

Danny Dichio heads home against his former club.

Darren Ward takes on Scott Dobie.

successive win, had a couple of chances to level before the break, but Andy Marshall made two athletic saves to deny them, tipping over Delroy Facey's volley and keeping out a Darren Moore header.

The dismissal of Koumas a couple of minutes before the interval for a second clumsy challenge on Wise resulted in a tactical substitution by Megson, which ultimately paid off handsomely.

On came Lloyd Dyer and Scott Dobie for James O'Connor and Facey, and the two subs combined for Johnson's 55th-minute leveller.

Dyer skipped down the left and crossed for Dobie, whose side-footed effort was finished by Johnson from barely a yard out.

Dyer nearly handed West Brom the lead just two minutes later, with a rasping left-foot drive that rattled the woodwork with Marshall stranded.

The Lions then woke from their second-half slumber, with the introduction of Peter Sweeney and then Neil Harris adding some pace and width.

Andy Roberts forced Hoult into a smart save from distance, Dichio fired over the bar and Sweeney was also denied by the visiting keeper.

The Lions continued to press for the winner, Wise firing a 30-yard drive wide before Dichio's flicked header was grasped on the line by the increasingly busy Hoult.

But despite the late dismissal of Danish defender Gaardsoe, Millwall just couldn't find a way through a resilient West Brom rearguard.

League Table	P	W	D	L	F	A	Pts
5 Sheff Utd	42	19	9	14	60	51	66
6 Wigan	41	17	14	10	55	42	65
7 Millwall	**41**	**17**	**14**	**10**	**51**	**41**	**65**
8 West Ham	42	16	16	10	58	44	64
9 C Palace	41	18	9	14	63	56	63

❝ Ray Wilkins

I couldn't see what happened from where I was but the lads said the foul was inside the box and it should have been a penalty. With those sort of decisions you win some and you lose some. We lost this one, but I have to be honest and say it was a very soft decision.

❞

Fixture Type: **Division One**

Date: **Sat, 17th April 2004**

Venue: **City Ground**

Attendance: **22,263**

Referee: **B.Curson**

NOTTINGHAM FOREST 2

MILLWALL 2

Form coming into fixture

NOTTM F	MILLWALL
WWDD	DDLD

Gerrard

Impey Dawson Morgan Rogers

Jess Evans Williams Reid

King Johnson

Harris Dichio

Cahill

Wise Ifill

Elliott

Livermore Ward Lawrence Ryan

Marshall

Doig	Sweeney
Sonner	Chadwick
Roche	McCammon
Robertson	Gueret
Westcarr	Hearn

Mark McCammon holds off Michael Dawson.

Substitute Nick Chadwick grabbed a dramatic late leveller as The Lions secured a valuable point in this epic City Ground clash.

After a fairly uneventful first half, the game sprang to life when Dave Livermore opened his account for the season seconds after the restart, only for Andy Reid to thump home a 55th-minute equaliser.

Wes Morgan and Danny Dichio were then shown straight red cards following an unnecessary 64th-minute altercation – which would cost Dichio a place in the FA Cup final – before David Johnson fired Forest's second on 70 minutes.

But with the clock ticking away and The Lions staring defeat in the face, up popped Chadwick with a crucial 84th-minute effort to keep Millwall's Play-Off dream alive.

Few among the 22,283 City Ground crowd could have imagined that the match would take such a dramatic turn following a first 45 minutes in which neither side managed to get going.

Neil Harris and Dichio combined well on the left to create an early opening for Wise, but his 18-yard effort flashed wide.

Just short of the quarter-hour, a sliced Andy Impey shot briefly

Statistics

Season	Fixture		Fixture	Season
257	4	Shots On Target	2	214
227	7	Shots Off Target	4	175
10	1	Hit Woodwork	0	6
142	5	Caught Offside	3	140
272	7	Corners	4	219
547	14	Fouls	18	653

Nick Chadwick celebrates his late equaliser.

	Event Line
	HALF TIME 0-0
46	Livermore (Direct Free Kick)
50	Evans (Dissent)
55	Reid (Open Play)
64	Morgan (Violent Conduct)
64	Dichio (Violent Conduct)
65	Williams (Off) Doig (On)
65	Harris (Off) Chadwick (On)
65	Ifill (Off) Sweeney (On)
70	Johnson (Open Play)
70	Wise (Dissent)
71	Jess (Ung Conduct)
74	Livermore (Foul)
76	Elliott (Off) McCammon (On)
82	Johnson (Off) Sonner (On)
84	Chadwick (Open Play)
	FULL TIME 2-2

threatened to cause Millwall keeper Andy Marshall problems before landing harmlessly on the roof of the net.

An Impey error at the other end moments later almost led to the opening score, as he stumbled and gifted possession to Harris, but the Millwall captain curled his shot wide.

Marshall did well to touch Marlon King's header onto the crossbar in the 25th minute. He followed that up with a strong save from Eoin Jess.

The action heated up as the second period began, Livermore's innocuous-looking free-kick floating in from the right and past the outstretched hands of Forest keeper Paul Gerrard.

Forest hauled themselves level nine minutes later when Reid strode past Marvin Elliott and hit a scorching 25-yarder that flew into the top corner.

Then came the dismissals, as Dichio and Morgan got involved in a pushing and shoving match that left referee Brian Curson with no option other than to show both players red cards.

Reid was lucky to escape punishment a couple of minutes later when he got a little too heavy in his own personal battle with Wise, and within seconds he'd laid the groundwork for Forest's second goal, passing to King, who centred for Johnson to net in the 70th minute.

With Millwall heading for defeat, there was one final twist to this amazing tale, as Chadwick latched onto a loose ball in the Forest box and lashed a rising effort into the top corner, for a late Lions leveller.

League Table	P	W	D	L	F	A	Pts
5 Wigan	43	18	15	10	59	43	69
6 West Ham	43	17	16	10	60	44	67
7 Millwall	42	17	15	10	53	43	66
8 Sheff Utd	43	19	9	15	60	52	66
9 C Palace	42	18	10	14	64	57	64

ff Ray Wilkins

I don't think we played particularly well. It was a bad day at the office, but the spirit was there once more and that's what got us through. We have been hit by injuries and today had Andy Roberts missing with a swollen knee. Robbie Ryan switched to right-back and did a solid job for us. We have to get on with it and use the players we have to the best of their ability.

ff

MILLWALL **1**

WATFORD **2**

Lee Cook struck a 71st-minute winner for Watford as Millwall's Play-Off hopes suffered a severe setback at The Den.

Danny Dichio's 16th-minute header looked like sending The Lions on their way to the three points which would have lifted them into the top six. But The Hornets turned the game on its head with two scores in a vibrant second-half display.

First, Darren Ward inadvertently steered the ball into his own net from close range while under pressure from Bruce Dyer. And then Cook crashed home an angled drive which gave home keeper Andy Marshall no chance.

The Lions' strong first-half performance suggested they were about to get back on track after five League games without a win. Dennis Wise's men sprayed the ball around accurately as they probed for any openings.

Their solid play was soon rewarded, as Peter Sweeney's free kick was knocked down by Nick Chadwick for Dichio to slot home with a diving header from close range.

Sweeney was again the provider two minutes later, but his cross from the byline was inches too high for Chadwick to get the downward header he needed.

Form coming into fixture

MILLWALL	WATFORD
DLDD	DWWD

Marshall

Ryan | Lawrence | Ward | Livermore

Wise

Ifill | Sweeney

Cahill

Dichio | Chadwick

Bouazza | Dyer

Cook | Hyde | Mahon | Devlin

Mayo | Gayle | Dyche | Baird

Chamberlain

Harris	Ardley
Elliott	Fitzgerald
Cogan	Pidgeley
Gueret	Doyley
McCammon	Vernazza

Statistics

Season	Fixture		Fixture	Season
218	4	Shots On Target	4	231
180	5	Shots Off Target	3	217
6	0	Hit Woodwork	1	9
144	4	Caught Offside	2	154
223	4	Corners	2	231
663	10	Fouls	7	567

Marvin Elliott controls under pressure.

Barry Cogan bursts forward.

Dichio headed just wide on the half hour before Paul Ifill produced a fine left-foot volley which fizzed narrowly off-target.

Whilst they had posed little attacking threat in the first half, Watford were a different side altogether after the break, equalising on 53 minutes when Paul Devlin knocked Cook's cross to the far post back across goal, only for Ward to put the ball into his own net. To be fair, Watford's Dyer could just as easily have got the vital touch.

Dyer looked to have put his side ahead on the hour, but his goal was disallowed.

The Hornets continued to press, and after Cook forced Marshall into a save on 66 minutes, he gave the Lions' keeper no chance with a sweet left-foot shot into the far corner five minutes later.

Millwall struggled to find a way through to the Watford goal, with sub Neil Harris' injury-time strike straight at Alec Chamberlain their first effort on target in the second half.

❝ Ray Wilkins

The guys are finding it difficult to come to terms with the Cup. They don't want to pick up any knocks. We played some very good football in the first half, but the lads were being very careful and this game was an amazing turn around.

❞

Event Line
16 ⚽ Dichio (Indirect Free-Kick)
40 ▢ Ifill (Foul)
HALF TIME 1-0
53 ⚽ Ward (Own Goal)
69 ⮂ Cahill (Off) Harris (On)
70 ⮂ Ifill (Off) Elliott (On)
71 ⚽ Cook (Open Play)
79 ⮂ Cook (Off) Ardley (On)
80 ⮂ Sweeney (Off) Cogan (On)
89 ⮂ Bouazza (Off) Fitzgerald (On)
FULL TIME 1-2

League Table	P	W	D	L	F	A	Pts
5 Wigan	43	18	15	10	59	43	69
6 West Ham	43	17	16	10	60	44	67
7 Millwall	43	17	15	11	54	45	66
8 Sheff Utd	43	19	9	15	60	52	66
9 C Palace	42	18	10	14	64	57	64

MILLWALL 0

READING 1

Form coming into fixture

MILLWALL	READING
LDDL	WLLD

Marshall

Elliott   Ward   Lawrence   Ryan

Wise

Ifill   Livermore

Chadwick

Dichio   McCammon

Kitson   Goater

Salako   Sidwell   Harper   Savage

Hughes   Newman   Williams   Murty

Ashdown

Harris	Morgan
Sweeney	Owusu
Gueret	Young
Hearn	Boucard
Braniff	Brooker

A home defeat to Reading left The Lions needing a miracle if they were to qualify for the Play-Offs.

Former Manchester City hitman Shaun Goater struck the winner with a sublime finish from John Salako's corner on 16 minutes.

Millwall, now four points off sixth position, went agonisingly close to stealing a point when Peter Sweeney's last-minute free kick smacked the woodwork.

The Lions started brightly, a neat build-up involving Paul Ifill and Mark McCammon ending with Danny Dichio chesting the ball down for Dennis Wise, whose fierce shot was deflected for a corner.

At the other end, it took the superb reflexes of Andy Marshall to deny Adrian Williams the opener on nine minutes. Salako delivered a dangerous corner, and after striker Dave Kitson's initial effort was blocked by Dichio, defender Williams hit a spectacular overhead kick that Marshall somehow tipped over the bar.

But the visitors didn't have to wait long before breaking the deadlock, as Salako swung in a corner to Goater, who had time to pick his spot with a 16th-minute volley.

A quick free kick from Wise almost caught the visitors out when Ifill ghosted in, but Kitson got back to clear the danger.

Iffs went close to levelling three minutes before the break with a blistering 25-yarder that Jamie Ashdown tipped on to the post.

Seconds before the break, The Lions introduced Neil Harris for Dichio, who was suffering with a back injury. Wise then replaced

Statistics

Season	Fixture		Fixture	Season
221	3	Shots On Target	2	219
184	4	Shots Off Target	3	206
8	2	Hit Woodwork	0	6
145	1	Caught Offside	0	159
229	6	Corners	5	246
672	9	Fouls	12	489

Nick Chadwick gets tangled up with James Harper.

Paul Ifill breaks forward.

Event Line		
16 ⚽ Goater (Corner)		
HALF TIME 0-1		
46 Dichio (Off) Harris (On)		
58 Wise (Foul)		
66 McCammon (Off) Sweeney (On)		
73 Savage (Off) Morgan (On)		
81 Goater (Off) Owusu (On)		
90 Newman (Foul)		
FULL TIME 0-1		

League Table	P	W	D	L	F	A	Pts
8 Sheff Utd	44	20	9	15	61	52	69
9 Reading	44	19	10	15	54	56	67
10 Millwall	44	17	15	12	54	46	66
11 Cardiff	44	17	12	15	66	56	63
12 Coventry	44	15	14	15	60	51	59

❝ Ray Wilkins

Everybody is very disappointed in the dressing room. We didn't create many chances in that game even though the lads worked hard. We now have to pick ourselves up on Monday and take a positive attitude into the last two League games, because we can't go into the FA Cup Final on a losing streak. ❞

❝ Darren Ward

It wasn't this defeat that has affected our hopes of reaching the Play-Offs, it was the games leading up to it that have. It's our own fault. ❞

McCammon with Sweeney on 66 minutes in a bid to find a way through a well-organised Reading rearguard.

Sweeney nearly made a dream start with his first touch, a rasping left-footer which flew narrowly over the bar.

Ifill was then inches from connecting with Nick Chadwick's tantalising ball across the face of goal.

The closest Wise's men came to an equaliser was in the 90th minute, when Sweeney's curling 20-yard free kick cannoned off the post.

Clearly, it just wasn't Millwall's day.

DERBY COUNTY 2

MILLWALL 0

Form coming into fixture

DERBY COUNTY	MILLWALL
DWWL	DDLL

Grant

Kenna Mawene Johnson Jackson

Tudgay Taylor Huddlestone Reich

Manel Peschisolido

Harris Sutton

Braniff

Livermore Ifill

Hearn

Ryan Ward Lawrence Elliott

Marshall

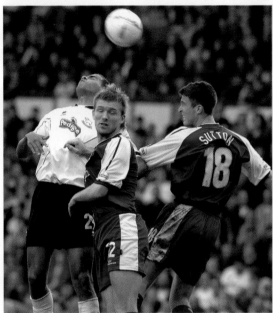

Darren Ward and John Sutton challenge with Tom Huddlestone.

Bolder	Sweeney
Holmes	Chadwick
Junior	Cogan
Oakes	Gueret
Mills	McCammon

Statistics

Season	Fixture		Fixture	Season
267	7	Shots On Target	2	223
237	7	Shots Off Target	6	190
8	0	Hit Woodwork	0	8
142	2	Caught Offside	9	154
245	5	Corners	4	233
600	21	Fouls	15	687

Millwall's slim hopes of reaching the Play-Offs were shattered as Derby ensured their First Division survival with stunning strikes in either half from Adam Bolder and Marco Reich.

It proved to be a bitterly disappointing afternoon for the lacklustre Lions, who failed to register a single shot on target during 90 frustrating minutes in which Andy Marshall denied the Rams a further goal with an excellent first-half penalty save from Ian Taylor.

The decision by referee Mark Cowburn to penalise Robbie Ryan for a "foul" on Marcus Tudgay after 17 minutes – and then add insult to injury by booking the Millwall man – was the first of a host of inaccurate calls by the official which infuriated players and fans alike.

On this occasion, justice was at least seen to be done when Taylor's well-struck spot kick was superbly tipped away by Marshall. Tudgay's free header from the resulting corner flashed wide as County continued to press for an opening goal.

The Lions, fielding a patched-up side that included a first full start for John Sutton alongside the recalled Neil Harris, plus Charley Hearn and Kevin Braniff in midfield, struggled to get going.

David Livermore shrugs off a challenge.

Event Line

17	▯	Ryan (Foul)
32	⇄	Johnson (Off) Bolder (On)
40	⊙	Bolder (Open Play)

HALF TIME 1-0

46	⇄	Braniff (Off) Sweeney (On)
46	▯	Hearn (Foul)
55	⇄	Harris (Off) Chadwick (On)
61	▯	Jackson (Foul)
69	⇄	Hearn (Off) Cogan (On)
72	⊙	Reich (Direct Free-Kick)
78	⇄	Reich (Off) Holmes (On)
87	⇄	Manel (Off) Junior (On)

FULL TIME 2-0

League Table	P	W	D	L	F	A	Pts
8 Sheff Utd	45	20	10	15	62	53	70
9 Reading	45	20	10	15	55	56	70
10 Millwall	45	17	15	13	54	48	66
11 Cardiff	45	17	13	15	67	57	64
12 Coventry	45	16	14	15	65	53	62

Derby, meanwhile, were energised by a 26,000-strong Pride Park crowd that got behind their team from the off, playing their part in making it difficult for Dennis Wise's men to settle.

It always looked like it would be The Rams who would break the deadlock, and they finally did in the 40th minute. Hearn was caught in possession by sub Bolder, who latched onto the ball and lashed a fearsome 22-yard drive that gave Marshall no chance.

Tom Huddlestone went close to increasing County's advantage as he fired over the bar, and only a timely tackle by Ryan on Manuel Manel denied the Rams' striker a clear shot on goal as the home side finished the half strongly.

As the second half began, Derby came flying out of the traps once again, full of purpose and power.

Manel, who had earlier wasted a glorious opportunity by firing into the side netting, was denied shortly after the restart when Marshall blocked his effort at the second attempt.

When The Rams eventually notched their second on 72 minutes, it owed as much to the ineptitude of referee Cowburn as the vision and precision of German midfielder Reich.

Matt Lawrence won the ball with a clean challenge on Derby striker Paul Peschisolido just outside the danger zone, but Mr Cowburn decided to stop play and award a free kick for an infringement that no one else seemed to notice. Reich stepped up and fired home with a quality finish that killed off not only the match, but also any remote chance The Lions had of sneaking a Play-Off spot.

❝ Dennis Wise

I was very disappointed particularly with one or two of our more experienced players. We had to throw in a number of youngsters who tried hard, but I expected a little bit more from some of the more senior members of the team. The back four did OK and Marvin Elliott showed just what an excellent player he is going to be, but there wasn't too much else to take from this performance.
❞

MILLWALL 1

BRADFORD CITY 0

Neil Harris kept his cool to fire a 58th-minute penalty against Bradford at The Den, as Millwall recorded a morale-boosting first League win in nine games.

Chopper's strike settled a tightly fought encounter in which Joe Dolan made a welcome to return to senior action and teenage midfielder Curtis Weston was handed his Lions first-team debut.

The game had that "end of season" feel about it at times, with The Bantams already relegated and Dennis Wise's men out of the Play-Off picture, but wanting to get back to winning ways ahead of the FA Cup Final.

In an evenly contested opening half, Tim Cahill nearly marked his return from suspension with a goal on nine minutes. Peter Sweeney

Form coming into fixture

MILLWALL	BRADFORD C
DLLL	LLLL

Marshall

Elliott Lawrence Ward Ryan

Ifill Cahill Livermore Sweeney

Sutton Harris

Branch Cadamarteri

Sanasy Wolleaston Penford Heckingbottom

Bower Gavin Wetherall Jacobs

Combe

Cogan Edds
Dolan Forrest
Weston Emanuel
Gueret Paston
McCammon Kearney

Debutant Curtis Weston controls the ball.

Statistics

Season	Fixture		Fixture	Season
227	4	Shots On Target	0	225
191	1	Shots Off Target	5	227
8	0	Hit Woodwork	0	5
158	4	Caught Offside	1	156
241	8	Corners	1	254
701	14	Fouls	16	626

Joe Dolan clears.

tried to slip the ball through to Harris, but Cahill intervened and charged through the heart of the visiting defence, only to be thwarted by the bravery of keeper Alan Combe. Cahill also saw his 41st-minute cross-shot well held by Combe.

Bradford's only noteworthy effort came after 25 minutes when Michael Branch lashed over from 20 yards.

Wise introduced Barry Cogan for John Sutton at half time, and the slight young Irishman staked his claim for a place in the FA Cup Final squad with an enterprising display which belied his tender years.

The same could be said for Marvin Elliott, who was again outstanding in his unfamiliar right-back role, despite the overzealous attention of City's Branch.

But it took the experienced head of striker Harris to settle this match, slotting home from the spot after Paul Heckingbottom had clearly handled in the area.

Promising midfielder Weston entered the game shortly afterwards and got straight into the action with a couple of crunching challenges. He was clearly determined to make an impression.

Big defender Dolan also clearly relished his outing, as he made some strong tackles, including a superb last-ditch interception as Branch prepared to shoot.

The Lions went close to a second when Cahill worked an opening and laid the ball off for Chopper, who fired over.

❝ Dennis Wise

It was important to get a win to boost our confidence a bit, and it's always good to finish the season on a high note. I would have liked a couple more goals, but it was nice to see youngsters like Curtis Weston and Barry Cogan out there, and they gave us a bit more energy in the second half. I was pleased too for big Joe Dolan, because it's been a long wait for him.

❞

MANCHESTER UNITED　　3

MILLWALL　　0

Statistics		
6	Shots On Target	1
7	Shots Off Target	4
0	Hit Woodwork	0
3	Caught Offside	2
7	Corners	2
11	Fouls	19

So, it turned out that the bookies were right to make Millwall 10-1 or thereabouts to cause the biggest FA Cup Final upset of all time.

But that didn't stop 21,000 Lions fans making it a party to remember at the Millennium Stadium.

Certainly it was the blue and white hordes who won the day in terms of singing the longest and loudest for their team, and although the difference in class between the sides told in the end, Dennis Wise's men did them proud.

Millwall kept the red tide at bay for almost the entire first half, with Andy Marshall pulling off a superb save to deny United skipper Roy Keane's volley, and Darren Ward clearing off the line from Cristiano Ronaldo.

The Lions forced a couple of corners, but in spite of the odd promising run from Paul Ifill, were unable to find a way through to Tim Howard.

The Lions make their entrance.

```
                    Howard
        G.Neville   Brown    Silvestre   O'Shea
        Ronaldo    Fletcher   Keane      Giggs
                    Scholes
                        van Nistelrooy
                    Harris
      Sweeney  Livermore  Wise   Cahill   Ifill
        Ryan       Ward   Lawrence   Elliott
                    Marshall
```

Carroll   Dunne
P.Neville   Cogan
Butt   Weston
Solskjaer   McCammon
Djemba-Djemba   Gueret

Event Line

44 ⚽ Ronaldo (Open Play)

Half-Time Score 1-0

49 ▢ Wise (Foul)

65 ⚽ van Nistelrooy (Penalty)

74 ⇄ Ryan (Off) Cogan (On)

75 ⇄ Harris (Off) McCammon (On)

81 ⚽ van Nistelrooy (Open Play)

84 ⇄ Fletcher (Off) Butt (On)

84 ⇄ Ronaldo (Off) Solskjaer (On)

84 ⇄ Howard (Off) Carroll (On)

89 ⇄ Wise (Off) Weston (On)

Full-Time Score 3-0

David Livermore controls, with Roy Keane lurking.

United finally got their noses in front a minute before the break when Ronaldo headed home from Gary Neville's cross. The second and third goals had a touch of controversy about them.

Firstly, United were awarded a penalty, despite Dave Livermore appearing to get a touch to the ball in a challenge on Ryan Giggs. Ruud van Nistelrooy rammed home from the spot.

And the Dutchman did it again on 81 minutes, converting Giggs' cross from an apparently offside position.

The scoreline might have read 3-0, but everyone in blue and white – both on the field and in the stands – went away a winner.

❛❛ Neil Harris

The players feel very privileged to have represented the club in their first FA Cup Final. It's been a massive effort by everybody at the club, not least the fans who have supported us from the Third Round onwards. It makes us feel very honoured to be part of this football club at this time. ❜❜

❛❛ Dennis Wise

We had a lot of youngsters out there, and I told them they should be proud of themselves. They've done fantastically well, and if it had been 0-0 at half-time, it might have been a different game. ❜❜

There Were
3 Wise Men
Only
1 Little Den

CONGRATULATIONS
MILLWALL
F.A. CUP FINALISTS 2004

KINGS FERRY

AFY 184X

End of Season Review

Division One Table

		P	W	D	L	F	A	GD	Pts
1	Norwich City	46	28	10	8	79	39	40	94
2	West Brom	46	25	11	10	64	42	22	86
3	Sunderland	46	22	13	11	62	45	17	79
4	West Ham United	46	19	17	10	67	45	22	74
5	Ipswich Town	46	21	10	15	84	72	12	73
6	Crystal Palace	46	21	10	15	72	61	11	73
7	Wigan Athletic	46	18	17	11	60	45	15	71
8	Sheffield United	46	20	11	15	65	56	9	71
9	Reading	46	20	10	16	55	57	-2	70
10	**Millwall**	**46**	**18**	**15**	**13**	**55**	**48**	**7**	**69**
11	Stoke City	46	18	12	16	58	55	3	66
12	Coventry City	46	17	14	15	67	54	13	65
13	Cardiff City	46	17	14	15	68	58	10	65
14	Nottingham Forest	46	15	15	16	61	58	3	60
15	Preston North End	46	15	14	17	69	71	-2	59
16	Watford	46	15	12	19	54	68	-14	57
17	Rotherham United	46	13	15	18	53	61	-8	54
18	Crewe Alexandra	46	14	11	21	57	66	-9	53
19	Burnley	46	13	14	19	60	77	-17	53
20	Derby County	46	13	13	20	53	67	-14	52
21	Gillingham	46	14	9	23	48	67	-19	51
22	Walsall	46	13	12	21	45	65	-20	51
23	Bradford City	46	10	6	30	38	69	-31	36
24	Wimbledon	46	8	5	33	41	89	-48	29

Division One Statistics

03/04		02/03
227	Shots On Target	270
191	Shots Off Target	261
8	Hit Woodwork	15
158	Caught Offside	208
241	Corners	245
16	Clean Sheets	13
1	Own Goals For	0
2	Own Goals Against	2

F	A	Goals Resulting From	F	A
35	34	Open Play	39	49
20	14	Set Piece	20	20

F	A	How Goals Were Scored	F	A
21	27	Right Foot	34	36
15	14	Left Foot	14	18
19	7	Header	11	15

F	A	When Goals Were Scored	F	A
23	20	First Half	25	32
32	28	Second Half	34	37

Season Progression Chart

Win: ■ Draw: ■ Loss: ■ League Position: 🔾 League Position 2002-03: 🔾 (Home fixtures in red)

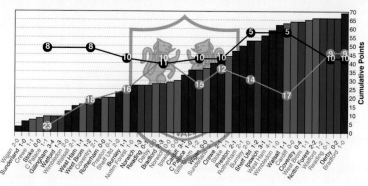

Neil Harris

Tim Cahill

03/04	Player Stats	02/03
38	Appearances	40
9	Goals	12
5	Assists	8

H	A	Goals Resulting From	H	A
2	2	Open Play	4	4
4	1	Set Piece	2	2

How Goals Were Scored

7	Right Foot	6
1	Left Foot	2
1	Header	4

When Goals Were Scored

4	First Half	4
5	Second Half	8

03/04	Player Stats	02/03
40	Appearances	11
9	Goals	3
7	Assists	2

H	A	Goals Resulting From	H	A
1	5	Open Play	1	-
3	-	Set Piece	1	1

How Goals Were Scored

1	Right Foot	2
2	Left Foot	-
6	Header	1

When Goals Were Scored

2	First Half	-
7	Second Half	3

Lions in Europe

Following Millwall's first appearance in an FA Cup Final in May, the club are now on the verge of an historic venture into Europe.

By virtue of Manchester United's qualification for the Champions League, The Lions were guaranteed a UEFA Cup spot win or lose at the Millennium Stadium. Consequently, Millwall fans' celebrations on May 22nd were all the greater knowing that a big prize was already in store.

Dennis Wise's men take their place in the First Round proper of the competition, the draw for which is made on August 27th.

A total of 32 clubs enter the competition at that stage, joining a further 32 who have progressed through from the two Qualifying Rounds.

The First Round will be played on a home and away basis, with the first leg taking place the week beginning September 12th, and the second the week beginning September 27th.

The majority of UEFA Cup ties will be played on Thursday evenings.

Should Millwall be successful in their First Round tie, they will progress to the group stage. Each group will comprise five teams. Each team will play four games within the group, two at home and two away.

The top three teams from each group will progress to the knockout stages, where eight teams from the Champions League join the competition.

Priority for tickets for UEFA Cup ties will be given to Season Ticket holders followed by Members.

Tickets for away ties will be limited as clubs participating in the UEFA Cup are only obliged to allocate 5% of their ground capacity to the visitors.

All away travel to European ties and tickets for those games will only be available through the Millwall Ticket Office and Millwall's official travel partners.

Ticket Information

A Season Ticket makes real sense for those of you who attend matches here on a regular basis. Not only does it save you the bother of queuing for tickets week in week out, it guarantees your seat (or block) for big games, and of course gives you top priority for Cup tickets. For those of you considering travelling to UEFA Cup ties abroad, this may be essential if tickets prove to be limited.

Season Ticket forms can be downloaded from our website **www.millwallfc.co.uk**, by sending an SAE to **Ticket Office, Millwall FC, The Den, Zampa Road, London SE16 3LN** or by picking one up in person at the ground.

Millwall Supporters Club Memberships

Once again, being a Supporters Club Member is the only way you will be able to purchase tickets for away games. There will also be a limited number of home fixtures which will again be 'Members Only' and these will include high profile matches against Cardiff City, Leeds United and West Ham United. Priority will also be given to Members, after Season Ticket Holders, in purchasing tickets for big Cup matches. Our FA Cup run last season emphasised why being a Member can be such an advantage in this respect.

Membership forms can be downloaded from our website **www.millwallfc.co.uk**, by sending an SAE to **Ticket Office, Millwall FC, The Den, Zampa Road, London SE16 3LN** or by picking one up in person at the ground.

Ticket Prices 2004-05

Category 1 West/East Stand	Category 2 West/East Stand
Adult £26	Adult £23
Senior £16	Senior £13
Junior £13	Junior £11

West Lower	West Lower
Adult £23	Adult £21
Senior £14	Senior £11
Junior £10	Junior £8

Cold Blow Lane	Cold Blow Lane
Adult £19	Adult £17
Senior £12	Senior £10
Junior £10	Junior £7

Family Enclosure (Members Only)	Family Enclosure (Members Only)
Adult £19	Adult £17
Senior £12	Senior £9
Junior £9	Junior £6

The Ticket Office can be contacted:
by telephone **0207 231 9999**
or via email **tickets@millwallplc.com**

Millwall fans gather to watch the FA Cup Final at the Millennium Stadium.

Player/Manager - Dennis Wise

Personal Info

Position: **Midfielder**

Nationality: **English**

Date of Birth: **16/12/1966**

Height: **5' 6" (168cm)**

Weight: **10st 9lbs (67.64kg)**

Previous Clubs: **Wimbledon, Chelsea, Leicester City.**

Having started out as a youngster at Southampton, midfielder Dennis was picked up by former Wimbledon boss Dave Bassett in March 1985, and from there on his career blossomed.

Although The Dons were labelled as 'Route One' merchants, Wisey soon emerged as a fine passer of the ball, with his pinpoint deliveries providing the ammunition for Alan Cork and John Fashanu.

The Kensington-born player made over 150 senior starts for Wimbledon before Chelsea stepped in to snap him up for £1.6m in July 1990. And it was at Stamford Bridge that his qualities were further recognised, earning him 21 senior caps for England at international level.

His time with Chelsea proved to be trophy laden, and Wise emerged as the most successful captain in the club's history, skippering the side to FA, Worthington and European Cup Winner's Cup glory.

However all good things come to an end and when Leicester City came in with a £1.6m bid in June 2001, Wise's 11-year affair with The Blues was over.

Leicester proved to be a less memorable experience with The Foxes slipping out of the Premiership at the end of the 2001/2 season, and Wise leaving in controversial circumstances in the summer.

He initially signed a deal that tied him to The Den until the summer of 2004, but took over a new role as player/manager on 15th October 2003 and is clearly relishing the position.

Player Stats 2003-04

Competition	Apps	Subs	⚽	▢	▪
League	26	5	1	8	1
FA Cup	6	0	1	3	0
Total	31	5	2	11	1

Career History

Season	Club	Apps	Subs	⚽
02 - 03	Millwall	3	1	3
01 - 02	Leicester City	17	2	1
00 - 01	Chelsea	40	1	3
99 - 00	Chelsea	48	1	9
98 - 99	Chelsea	36	1	2
97 - 98	Chelsea	39	0	3
96 - 97	Chelsea	36	4	6
95 - 96	Chelsea	43	1	8
94 - 95	Chelsea	23	1	6
93 - 94	Chelsea	35	0	4
92 - 93	Chelsea	27	0	3
91 - 92	Chelsea	38	0	12

Matt Lawrence

Personal Info

Position: **Defender**

Nationality: **English**

Date of Birth: **19.06.1974**

Height: **6' 1" (185cm)**

Weight: **12st 12lbs (81.72kg)**

Previous Clubs: **Wycombe, Fulham**

Matt made a late entry into the professional ranks with Wycombe Wanderers, after taking a degree in American Literature in the United States whilst playing college football over there. Initially a midfielder, Matt largely operated at right-back following his £250,000 move to The Den in March 2000. He missed just one game on Millwall's march to the Second Division title, and was voted by the Lions fans as their Player of the Year in his first season.

The 2001/2 campaign started well for Matt, before he was sidelined with the after affects of concussion sustained at Gillingham on September 11th.

On his return to the team, he re-gained some of his best form for the club and linked up well with Paul Ifill on the right flank.

Matt fell out of favour with former boss Mark McGhee at the start of the 2003/4 campaign and looked to be on his way out of the club, but a change of manager combined with a switch to a central defensive role paid off handsomely.

Alongside Darren Ward, Matt has forged an outstanding partnership in the heart of defence, with his displays rewarded in the shape of a new contract that keeps Matt at The Den for another two seasons.

Player Stats 2003-04

Competition	Apps	Subs	⚽	▢	■
League	34	2	0	5	0
FA Cup	7	0	0	0	0
League Cup	1	0	0	1	0
Total	42	2	0	6	0

Career History

Season	Club	Apps	Subs	⚽
02-03	Millwall	36	2	0
01-02	Millwall	29	3	0
99-00	Millwall	52	0	0
98-99	Millwall	11	0	0
99-00	Wycombe	37	0	2
98-99	Fulham	1	1	0
98-99	Wycombe	51	0	0
97-98	Fulham	13	1	0
96-97	Wycombe	17	1	1
95-96	Wycombe	1	2	0

Tim Cahill

Personal Info

Position: **Midfielder**

Nationality: **Australian**

Date of Birth: **06.12.1979**

Height: **5' 10" (178cm)**

Weight: **10st 11lbs (68.55kg)**

Twice voted Millwall Young Player of the Year, the Aussie-born midfielder had a remarkable start to his career, appearing at Wembley at the age of 19 and scoring over 30 goals in his first three seasons as a senior – 13 of those coming in the 2001/2 campaign.

So determined was Tim to forge a career in professional football, that he left behind family and friends in Australia at the age of 16, travelling half-way around the world to try his luck in England. He has already been well rewarded and has the potential to go all the way to the top. A forceful, strong running midfielder, Tim is remarkably good in the air for a player of only average height.

Thanks to FIFA's rule change on eligibility, He was able to make his Australia debut in March 2004 against South Africa. Tim went on to score six goals in three matches, to ensure the Socceroos' made it to the next stage of qualifying for the 2006 World Cup.

Tim's performances and vital goals during the 2003/4 campaign drew rave reviews and no little attention from envious managers. In May, he became the third Aussie to appear in an FA Cup Final.

Player Stats 2003-04

Competition	Apps	Subs	⚽	▢	◼
League	40	0	9	16	2
FA Cup	7	0	3	1	0
League Cup	1	0	0	0	0
Total	48	0	12	17	2

Career History

Season	Club	Apps	Subs	⚽
02-03	Millwall	9	2	3
01-02	Millwall	49	0	13
00-01	Millwall	44	3	10
99-00	Millwall	50	0	12
98-99	Millwall	34	3	6
97-98	Millwall	1	0	0

6 Joe Dolan

Personal Info

Position: **Defender**

Nationality: **Northern Irish**

Date of Birth: **27.05.1980**

Height: **6' 3" (191cm)**

Weight: **13st 5lbs (84.9kg)**

Big centre-half Joe will be determined to make up for lost time, after suffering an horrific 18-months out through injury.

Having progressed through to senior level from the Millwall Youth team, Joe got his big chance in February 1999 when he was thrust into an Auto-Windscreens Shield Area Semi-Final against Gillingham.

He retained his place in the side, until he sustained a facial injury against Fulham the following April, having already played at Wembley at the age of 18.

The Northern Ireland Under-21 international suffered another injury setback, when he broke his left leg in a freak collision with team mate Robbie Ryan during the League encounter with Bristol Rovers at The Den on February 3rd 2001. He subsequently sustained knee ligament trouble shortly after returning to full training. After a 21-month lay-off Joe made an emotional return to first team action at Stoke in November 2002, but suffered a cruel blow at The Den a week later when, in a League game against Bradford City, he was stretchered off after damaging his cruciate knee ligament.

Joe battled back once again, and returned to reserve action at Crystal Palace in January 2004. He made it back into the first team for the final game of the season, appearing as a second-half substitute, ironically, against Bradford City.

Player Stats 2003-04

Competition	Apps	Subs	⚽	⬜	⬛
League	0	1	0	0	0
Total	0	1	0	0	0

Career History

Season	Club	Apps	Subs	⚽
02 - 03	Millwall	2	0	0
00 - 01	Millwall	27	0	2
99 - 00	Millwall	17	1	1
98 - 99	Millwall	9	0	1

⟨7⟩ Paul Ifill

Personal Info

Position: **Midfielder**

Nationality: **Barbadian**

Date of Birth: **20.08.1979**

Height: **6' 0" (183cm)**

Weight: **12st 9lbs (80.35kg)**

Paul has won over The Den faithful with his pace, trickery ball skills and unpredictability. Having started out as an out-and-out striker, he has successfully switched to a wide midfield role and is at his best running at opposing defences.

He has also improved his defensive responsibilities, as was proved on a number of occasions last season whilst making vital interceptions inside the danger zone.

A product of Millwall's successful youth system Paul came through the ranks alongside the likes of Tim Cahill, Steven Reid, Joe Dolan and Richard Sadlier. He now has 200 senior appearances for The Lions under his belt.

During the summer of 2004, Iffs earned international honours for the first time when he was selected by Barbados for two World Cup qualifiers against St Kitts & Nevis.

The 25-year-old Brighton born winger looks set to make a major impact in The Championship, as the old First Division will be known next season, and is relishing the challenge of European football.

Player Stats 2003-04

Competition	Apps	Subs	⊙	▢	▪
League	29	4	8	3	0
FA Cup	6	0	1	1	0
Total	35	4	9	4	0

Career History

Season	Club	Apps	Subs	⊙
02 - 03	Millwall	50	0	7
01 - 02	Millwall	32	13	4
00 - 01	Millwall	33	7	7
99 - 00	Millwall	41	6	11
98 - 99	Millwall	12	3	1

David Livermore

8

Personal Info

Position: **Midfielder**
Nationality: **English**
Date of Birth: **20/05/1980**
Height: **6' 0" (183cm)**
Weight: **12st 7lbs (79.45kg)**
Previous Clubs: **Arsenal**

One of the shrewdest Millwall purchases in recent seasons, costing just £30,000 from Arsenal in September 1999 following a loan spell. Livermore was a centre-back as a junior with the Gunners, but established himself as first choice in central midfield for Millwall after a spell filling in wide on the left. Livers plays with a maturity which belies his age, and his tackling and work rate are reminiscent of Terry Hurlock in his Millwall heyday.

Dave had the distinction of scoring the final Football League goal of the old millennium, being presented with a commemorative bottle of champagne for his injury time winner against Brentford on December 28th 1999. He made 39 appearances in the Championship winning side scoring three goals, and emerged as one of the teams outstanding performers in the 2001/2 promotion Play-Off run-in.

Last season Dave showed his strength and versatility, operating in a central and wide midfield role, adapting superbly at left-back in place of Robbie Ryan.

Livers, 24, has been one of Millwall's most consistent performers, and after more than 200 senior appearances for the club, no-one deserved the reward of an FA Cup Final appearance more than Dave.

Player Stats 2003-04

Competition	Apps	Subs	⊙	▢	▮
League	35	1	1	9	1
FA Cup	7	0	0	2	0
Total	42	1	1	11	1

Career History

Season	Club	Apps	Subs	⊙
02-03	Millwall	46	0	2
01-02	Millwall	49	0	0
00-01	Millwall	46	0	4
99-00	Millwall	33	3	2

Neil Harris

Personal Info

Position: **Striker**

Nationality: **English**

Date of Birth: **12.07.1977**

Height: **5' 11" (180cm)**

Weight: **12st 9lbs (80.35kg)**

Previous Clubs: **Cambridge City**

Chopper initially cost Millwall just £30,000 from non-League Cambridge City prior to the transfer deadline in 1998. Barely two years later, Harris established himself as one of the most feared marksmen outside the Premiership, scoring 25 League goals in 1999/2000 (the first Millwall player since Teddy Sheringham in 1991 to do so), and attracting offers of over £1million for his signature.

Neil signed a new-improved four year deal with Millwall in May 2000, and netted a further 28 goals in 2000/1, sharing the Division Two 'Golden Boot' with Jamie Cureton.

Less than a week after signing yet another improved deal came the bombshell news that Neil had testicular cancer, and following an operation he embarked on a course of radiotherapy treatment. He returned before Christmas, and scored a sensational goal in The Lions' 4-1 win at Watford on New Year's Day.

A former Liverpool triallist, Harris had been trailed by a number of League clubs, but it was Millwall who were most convinced of the striker's potential, which was revealed with 18 goals in his first full season, landing him the Player of the Year accolade in 1999/2000.

Articulate and intelligent, he worked for a Japanese bank prior to becoming a professional footballer – and he will be banking on bagging plenty of goals to help steer The Lions to the Premiership this season.

Player Stats 2003-04

Competition	Apps	Subs	⚽	☐	■
League	26	12	9	5	0
FA Cup	7	0	1	0	0
League Cup	1	0	0	0	0
Total	34	12	10	5	0

Career History

Season	Club	Apps	Subs	⚽
02 - 03	Millwall	35	6	12
01 - 02	Millwall	12	12	4
00 - 01	Millwall	45	3	28
99 - 00	Millwall	37	6	25
98 - 99	Millwall	37	3	15
97 - 98	Millwall	2	1	0

10 Danny Dichio

Personal Info

Position: **Striker**
Nationality: **English**
Date of Birth: **19.10.1974**
Height: **6' 3" (191cm)**
Weight: **12st 3lbs (77.63kg)**
Previous Clubs: **QPR, Sunderland, Sampdoria, Lecce, West Brom**

Danny made a big impact at The Den, after joining The Lions on loan from West Bromwich Albion in January 2004, scoring twice on his debut in the 2-1 win over Sunderland, and then repeating the feat a week later as Millwall beat Crewe by the same scoreline at Gresty Road.

'Dich' also headed the winner in the FA Cup Fifth Round victory over Burnley, after which the move became permanent, with a fee which could rise to £675,000.

The big striker began his career at Queens Park Rangers, playing 75 games for the Loftus Road outfit under Ray Wilkins. After a brief spell with Sampdoria and Lecce in Italy, he returned to England, spending four seasons at Sunderland before moving on to The Hawthorns.

Danny's 2003/4 campaign ended in heartbreak when he missed the FA Cup Final through suspension after being sent-off at Nottingham Forest.

The popular front man is now looking to make up for that disappointment by helping The Lions to promotion whilst enjoying some European glory in the UEFA Cup this season.

Player Stats 2003-04

Competition	Apps	Subs	⚽	▢	▮
League	15	0	7	5	1
FA Cup	5	0	1	2	0
Total	20	0	8	7	1

Career History

Season	Club	Apps	Subs	⚽
02-03	West Bromwich Albion	22	9	8
01-02	West Bromwich Albion	30	1	10
00-01	Sunderland	8	15	2
99-00	Sunderland	3	11	4
98-99	Sunderland	21	22	12
97-98	Sunderland	3	13	0
96-97	QPR	35	8	8
95-96	QPR	24	9	11
94-95	QPR	4	5	3
93-94	Barnet	9	0	2

33 Andy Marshall

Personal Info

Position: **Goalkeeper**

Nationality: **English**

Date of Birth: **14/04/1975**

Height: **6' 2" (188cm)**

Weight: **13st 7lbs (85.8kg)**

Previous Clubs: **Norwich City, Ipswich Town, Wolves**

Suffolk-born keeper Andy made 195 League appearances for Norwich City, before joining East Anglian rivals Ipswich Town on a Bosman-free transfer in 2001. He was virtually ever-present at Portman Road the season before last, but having lost his place to Kelvin Davis, and with his contract up in the summer, Marshall was keen to secure first team football elsewhere.

After a spell on loan at Wolves, he joined Millwall on a similar basis in January, following an injury to first choice keeper Tony Warner, and made his Lions debut at Crewe.

Andy played a key role in Millwall's run to the FA Cup Final, and put in fine displays in the Semi-Final and Final in particular.

The 29-year-old was delighted to make his move to The Den permanent, agreeing a two-year deal with Millwall on 8th July.

Player Stats 2003-04

Competition	Apps	Subs	⚽	☐	▮
League	16	0	0	0	0
FA Cup	4	0	0	0	0
Total	20	0	0	0	0

Career History

Season	Club	Apps	Subs	⚽
01-03	Ipswich Town	69	0	0
97-01	Norwich City	183	0	0
96-97	Bournemouth	10	0	0
96-97	Gillingham	5	0	0
94-97	Norwich City	30	0	0

Darren Ward

Personal Info

Position: **Defender**

Nationality: **English**

Date of Birth: **13/09/1978**

Height: **6' 3" (191cm)**

Weight: **12st 6lbs (78.99kg)**

Previous Clubs: **Watford, QPR**

A former trainee with Watford, Darren made his senior debut for The Hornets in 1995/6, but did not become a first team regular at Vicarage Road until the 2000/1 season.

However, he gained Premiership experience under Graham Taylor, and also had a spell on loan at QPR, before returning to establish himself in the Watford side. Following the arrival of Luca Vialli as manager, Darren found himself down the pecking order and consequently jumped at the chance to resurrect his career at Millwall, who paid a fee rising to £500,000 for his signature in early October.

Having made his debut at West Brom in a three-man defensive formation, Darren then had to be patient as the team reverted to a 4-4-2 system, with Nethercott and Dyche forming the first choice pairing. But Dyche's rib injury towards the end of the campaign handed Darren a first-team opening, and he grabbed the chance with some outstanding displays.

Wardy was ever-present during the 2003/4 campaign and his outstanding level of consistency was rewarded when he was voted Millwall's Player of the Year in May, followed by the award of a new three-year contract during the summer.

Player Stats 2003-04

Competition	Apps	Subs	⚽	▢	▮
League	46	0	3	5	0
FA Cup	7	0	0	0	0
League Cup	1	0	0	0	0
Total	54	0	3	5	0

Career History

Season	Club	Apps	Subs	⚽
02-03	Millwall	41	3	1
01-02	Watford	1	1	0
01-02	Millwall	13	4	0
00-01	Watford	46	0	2
99-00	QPR	15	0	0
99-00	Watford	7	2	1
98-99	Watford	1	0	0
96-97	Watford	8	0	0
95-96	Watford	1	0	0

The Chairman's Room is an exclusive Matchday Lounge for the 2004/2005 season.
This package offers you and your guests the opportunity to meet and chat with the Chairman or one of his fellow Directors prior to Kick-Off. Whether you are looking to entertain existing or prospective new clients the Chairman's Room will suit all your requirements.

Maximum number 12 persons

- Welcome drink on arrival
- Behind the scenes tour of the stadium
  (Saturdays only)
- Exclusive pay bar facility
- Complimentary matchday programme and team sheet for each guest
- A la Carte meal with wine
- Dedicated waitress service
- Seat in Directors Box
- Half-time refreshments
- Full-time refreshments
- Souvenir gift for each guest
- Exclusive Man of the Match presentation with a framed signed team photograph
- Photograph of your sponsors party
- 1/2 page advert in the matchday programme
- Company logo on front of the programme
- Scoreboard and tannoy acknowledgments
- Two car parking spaces *(subject to availability)*

PRICE £2500 + VAT
for a maximum of 12 people

The Chairman's Room

Millwall Football Club

For further information contact
Matchday Hospitality on 0207 740 0501

Kevin Muscat

Experienced defender Muscat was snapped up by Millwall on a free transfer from Scottish giants Glasgow Rangers at the end of August 2003. The Blackburn-born utility man had enjoyed spells with Palace and Wolves before moving north of the border.

Excellent going forward and a strong tackler, Muzzy's achilles heel has been his disciplinary record. After being red carded in only his second game for The Lions at Watford, the Australian international pledged to harness his natural aggression in a positive way for the benefit of the team.

Such was his success in achieving this that he was made captain of the side in succession to Stuart Nethercott and became an influential player both on and off the pitch during the campaign.

Unfortunately, Muzzy sustained a serious knee injury during the FA Cup Semi-Final against Sunderland which spelt the end of his season and cost him a place in the Final against Manchester United. One small compensation was the honour of leading the team out at the Millennium Stadium alongside Tony Warner.

Kevin is expected to be back in first team action in the autumn.

Player Stats 2003-04

Competition	Apps	Subs	⚽	▢	◼
League	27	0	0	6	2
FA Cup	6	0	0	1	0
Total	33	0	0	7	2

Career History

Season	Club	Apps	Subs	⚽
02-03	Rangers	26	2	0
01-02	Wolverhampton	38	0	0
00-01	Wolverhampton	42	0	4
99-00	Wolverhampton	49	0	4
98-99	Wolverhampton	43	0	4
97-98	Crystal Palace	10	0	0
97-98	Wolverhampton	27	2	3
96-97	Crystal Palace	49	2	2

Kevin Braniff

Personal Info

Position: **Striker**

Nationality: **Irish**

Date of Birth: **04.03.1983**

Height: **5' 11" (180cm)**

Weight: **10st 10lbs (68.1kg)**

Northern Ireland U21 international, Kevin made his first team debut on August 22nd 2000, scoring a wonder goal in a 2-1 League Cup tie at Brighton. He went on to make five League appearances plus four in the League Cup in the 2000/1 season, but his opportunities were restricted to just a handful of appearances on the bench last term.

However, Bran slowly but surely established himself as a regular in the first team squad, scoring vital goals against Nottingham Forest and Walsall during 2003/4. He begins the new season on loan to Rushden & Diamonds to play regular first team football before returning to The Den after three months.

Player Stats 2003-04

Competition	Apps	Subs	⚽	▢	▪
League	6	10	1	2	0
FA Cup	1	3	1	0	0
League Cup	0	1	0	0	0
Total	7	14	2	2	0

Career History

Season	Club	Apps	Subs	⚽
02-03	Millwall	6	6	0
01-02	Millwall	0	2	0
00-01	Millwall	5	5	1

〈23〉 Mark McCammon

Personal Info

Position: **Striker**

Nationality: **Barbadian**

Date of Birth: **07/08/1978**

Height: **6' 5" (196cm)**

Weight: **14st 5lbs (91.25kg)**

Previous Clubs: **Cambridge Utd, Charlton, Swindon, Brentford**

Mark was signed by Brentford during the 2000 close season. Formerly a non-contract player with Cambridge United, he earned himself a contract with the then First Division Champions Charlton following an impressive trial period, in which he scored seven goals in ten reserve team outings.

Mark initially signed for The Lions on March 27th 2003, on contract until the end of the 2002/3 season, but did so well he was subsequently snapped up on a two-year deal.

Already friendly with several members of The Lions squad, and having played for a short period with Neil Harris at Cambridge City, Mark sustained a serious knee injury in the final match of the 2002/3 campaign.

He returned to action for the reserves in late January 2004.

He went on to feature regularly in the first team squad to the end of the season and made a substitute's appearance in the FA Cup Final against Manchester United.

Mark was also called up by Barbados in June for their World Cup qualifiers against St Kitts & Nevis.

Player Stats 2003-04

Competition	Apps	Subs	⚽	▢	▮
League	3	3	0	0	0
FA Cup	0	1	0	0	0
Total	3	4	0	0	0

Career History

Season	Club	Apps	Subs	⚽
01-02	Brentford	35	6	8
00-01	Millwall	7	0	2
99-00	Brentford	1	15	0
98-99	Brentford	17	10	4
97-98	Charlton Athletic	1	4	0
96-97	Swindon Town	4	0	0
95-96	Cambridge United	1	1	0
95-96	Cambridge United	0	2	0

Marvin Elliott

Personal Info

Position: **Midfielder**

Nationality: **English**

Date of Birth: **15/09/1984**

Height: **6' 0" (183cm)**

Weight: **12st 2lbs (77.18kg)**

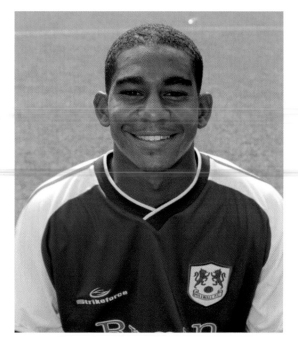

A powerful midfielder, who forced his way into Mark McGhee's first team plans towards the end of the 2002/3 campaign, and has emerged as a consistent member of Dennis Wise's squad.

The 19-year-old made his debut as a second-half sub at Nottingham Forest in the penultimate game of the 2002/3, and marked his first full appearance for The Lions in December 2003, with a Man of the Match winning display in a 3-1 success at Cardiff City.

Marvin established himself as a regular in the side during the second half of the season, and his adaptability was amply demonstrated when he filled in as a makeshift right back in the absence of Kevin Muscat and Andy Roberts. His performance in what was not his natural position in the FA Cup Final against Manchester United earned him rave reviews.

Player Stats 2003-04

Competition	Apps	Subs	⊙	☐	■
League	14	7	0	1	0
FA Cup	1	3	0	0	0
Total	15	10	0	1	0

Career History

Season	Club	Apps	Subs	⊙
02-03	Millwall	0	1	0

Personal Info

Position: **Midfielder**

Nationality: **Scottish**

Date of Birth: **25/09/1984**

Height: **6' 0" (183cm)**

Weight: **12st 11lbs (81.26kg)**

Left-sided midfielder Peter made his debut for the Under-17s at Watford on 27th February 1999, and has gone on to record over 50 appearances at U17 and U19 level, before progressing through the reserves to the first team.

Such was the quality of his performances for the reserves, that he went on to make his debut as a substitute in the 2-1 home defeat by Sheffield Wednesday in March 2002, and emerged as a pivotal figure in Dennis Wise's team selections during the 2003/4 campaign.

Peter joined the club as a 14-year-old, and played one season in the highly successful U15s side. He has gained representative honours at County and District level and played for England schoolboys.

However, the fact that he was born in Glasgow of Scottish parents means that Peter will in future play for Scotland, for whom he has already gained several caps at U21s level.

Player Stats 2003-04

Competition	Apps	Subs	⚽	▢	▮
League	21	8	2	2	0
FA Cup	2	3	0	0	0
Total	23	11	2	2	0

Career History

Season	Club	Apps	Subs	⚽
02-03	Millwall	1	5	1
01-02	Millwall	0	1	0

Celebrating a special occasion such as a 21st or 40th Birthday, or Anniversary and stuck for ideas on what to do?

Why not celebrate with our
New Celebration Package

- Drinks Reception on arrival
- Behind the scenes stadium tour *(Saturday only)*
- Three course meal with wine
- Table Decorations (balloons & streamers)
- Match Programme & team sheet for each guest
- Programme, Scoreboard & Tannoy acknowledgments
- Executive Area seats for the match
- Use of the exclusive Sponsors Lounge
- Half-time & Full-time refreshments
- Pay bar facilities available
- Souvenir gift
- Dedicated waitress service
- Millwall Celebration Cake & Bottle of Champagne
- Opportunity to vote for Sponsors' Man of the Match
- Presentation photograph with the Man of the Match
- Signed Millwall Football
- Car parking space *(subject to availability)*

This package is for a minimum of 8 people

ADULTS £75 +VAT per person
JUNIORS £45 per person (16 & Under)

DON'T FORGET, if you are an existing Season Ticket Holder or Executive Club Member, your current status will entitle you to a discount if you book a Matchday Hospitality Package for any of our home League games.

Millwall Football Club

For further information contact
Matchday Hospitality on 0207 740 0501

Alan Dunne

Right-back Alan has suffered a frustrating time with injuries, including a fractured ankle that ruined his 2002/3 season.

A regular for the reserves, he made his senior debut at Sheffield United in March 2002, and in spite of further appearances at first team level last term, injury has intervened whenever he seems to be on the verge of establishing himself.

Player Stats 2003-04

Competition	Apps	Subs	⚽	▢	■
League	4	4	0	1	0
League Cup	0	1	0	0	0
Total	4	5	0	1	0

Personal Info

Position: **Defender**

Nationality: **Irish**

Date of Birth: **23.08.1982**

Height: **5' 10" (178cm)**

Weight: **11st 1lbs (70.37kg)**

Career History

Season	Club	Apps	Subs	⚽
02-03	Millwall	3	1	0
01-02	Millwall	0	1	0

28 Mark Phillips

Another product of the Youth Academy who has broken through to first team level, Mark made his senior debut at right back against Preston on September 15th 2001. Although more accustomed to playing centre-back, such is his versatility that he has played as a striker for both reserve and youth sides and has captained both. A succession of niggly injuries wrecked the 2003/4 campaign, but he was awarded a new one-year contract.

Player Stats 2003-04

Competition	Apps	Subs	⚽	▢	■
League Cup	0	1	0	0	0
Total	0	1	0	0	0

Personal Info

Position: **Defender**

Nationality: **English**

Date of Birth: **27/01/1982**

Height: **6' 2" (188cm)**

Weight: **11st 2lbs (70.82kg)**

Career History

Season	Club	Apps	Subs	⚽
02-03	Millwall	8	0	0
01-02	Millwall	1	0	0

Bob Peeters

At 6ft 5in tall, striker Peeters is a thoughtful player who holds the ball up well and brings others into play. Joining Millwall for an undisclosed fee from Vitesse Arnheim in August, he bagged three goals in his first four appearances. Belgian Bob has won 12 full caps for his country, scoring four goals, and a Belgian championship medal with local club Lierse.

Player Stats 2003-04

Competition	Apps	Subs	⚽	☐	▮
League	16	4	3	4	0
Total	16	4	3	4	0

Personal Info

Position: **Striker**

Nationality: **Belgian**

Date of Birth: **10/01/1974**

Height: **6' 5" (196cm)**

Weight: **13st 8lbs (86.0kg)**

Career History

Season	Club	Apps	Subs	⚽
02-03	Vitesse	29	4	10
01-02	Vitesse	9	6	2
00-01	Vitesse	32	3	10

Charley Hearn

Very promising midfielder who made his senior debut at Walsall on September 29th 2001, when he came on as a second-half substitute at the age of 17. He was selected by 'The Sun' newspaper on January 1st 2000 as one of their promising young sportsmen/women for the new millennium, and will be hoping to live up to that expectation.

Player Stats 2003-04

Competition	Apps	Subs	⚽	☐	▮
League	3	4	0	1	0
League Cup	1	0	0	0	0
Total	4	4	0	1	0

Personal Info

Position: **Striker**

Nationality: **English**

Date of Birth: **05/11/1983**

Height: **5' 10" (178cm)**

Weight: **12st (76.27kg)**

Career History

Season	Club	Apps	Subs	⚽
02-03	Millwall	8	6	0
01-02	Millwall	0	2	0

◄32► Ben May

Ben scored on his Academy League debut for the U17s, in 2000 at Blackburn Rovers, finishing the season as top scorer (13 league goals). His full senior debut was at Gillingham in August 2002, and he scored his first League goal the following week at home to Ipswich Town. Ben spent the 2003/4 season at Brentford on loan, showing a remarkable degree of promise, assurance, and confidence.

Player Stats 2003-04

Competition	Apps	Subs	⚽	▢	▮
League	38	3	7	7	0
FA Cup	1	0	0	0	0
Total	39	3	7	7	0

Personal Info

Position: **Striker**

Nationality: **English**

Date of Birth: **10/03/1984**

Height: **6' 1" (185cm)**

Weight: **12st 1lbs (76.73kg)**

Career History

Season	Club	Apps	Subs	⚽
02-03	Colchester	4	2	0
02-03	Millwall	5	7	1

◄11► Curtis Weston

Curtis is a feisty midfielder renowned for his tigerish tackling and keen eye for goal. A product of Millwall's Youth Academy, the 17-year-old forced his way into Dennis Wise's first team plans in the final Division One match of the 2003/4 season, making his first senior start as a second-half substitute.

He then went on to break into the record books, when he became the youngest player ever to appear in the FA Cup final, coming on as a last-minute substitute for Dennis Wise at the age of 17 and 119 days.

Personal Info

Position: **Midfielder**

Nationality: **English**

Date of Birth: **24/01/1987**

Height: **5' 10" (179cm)**

Weight: **11st 6lbs (72.57kg)**

Player Stats 2003-04

Competition	Apps	Subs	⚽	▢	▮
League	0	1	0	0	0
FA Cup	0	1	0	0	0
Total	0	1	0	0	0

Paul Robinson

34

Robbo made his senior debut against Cambridge United in the FA Cup Third Round in January 2003, coming on after five minutes for the injured Stuart Nethercott.

The following week, Paul made his first start and League debut against Watford at home, scoring his first goal for the club in a replay against Cambridge three days later.

Paul was one of the outstanding competitors of 2002/3 and continued his excellent form last campaign, until damaging his cruciate knee ligaments at Norwich City on 8th November.

Player Stats 2003-04

Competition	Apps	Subs	⚽	☐	■
League	7	2	0	0	0
Total	7	2	0	0	0

Personal Info

Position: **Defender**

Nationality: **English**

Date of Birth: **07/01/1982**

Height: **6' 1" (185cm)**

Weight: **11st 9lbs (74.0kg)**

Career History

Season	Club	Apps	Subs	⚽
02-03	Millwall	15	3	1

Tony Craig

35

Greenwich-born Tony, 19, came through the Millwall youth ranks to start his senior career in the final two games of 2002/3. He made his home debut in the last game of the season, rounding off his short campaign in style by scoring the first goal in The Lions' 2-0 victory against Coventry City. Hampered by a pelvic injury during the opening stages of the 2003/4 campaign, he is now aiming to re-establish himself in the first team picture.

Player Stats 2003-04

Competition	Apps	Subs	⚽	☐	■
League	0	3	0	0	0
FA Cup	0	1	0	0	0
Total	0	4	0	0	0

Personal Info

Position: **Defender**

Nationality: **Rep of Ireland**

Date of Birth: **20/04/1985**

Height: **6' 0" (183cm)**

Weight: **11st 10lbs (74.25kg)**

Career History

Season	Club	Apps	Subs	⚽
02-03	Millwall	2	0	1

◀ 38 ▶ Trevor Robinson

Pacey young winger Trevor featured regularly for the U19s and reserves last season, making such a good impression with his enthusiasm, pace and skill that he was called for his first team debut as a substitute at Cardiff City in December 2003.

Trevor came on for the last few minutes in Millwall's 3-1 win, and was inches away from marking his League debut with his very first touch of the ball - a rasping 20-yard drive that flashed narrowly wide of the target.

Player Stats 2003-04					
Competition	Apps	Subs	⚽	☐	◼
League	0	1	0	0	0
Total	0	1	0	0	0

Personal Info

Position: **Midfielder**

Nationality: **English**

Date of Birth: **20/09/1984**

Height: **5' 11" (181cm)**

Weight: **13st (83.0kg)**

◀ 39 ▶ Mark Quigley

Striker Quigley has emerged as one of the clubs brightest young prospects. A prolific scorer for the U17's and then U19's, Republic of Ireland U20 international Quigs has continued his excellent progress through the reserve team to the senior side, making his debut as a late substitute against Ipswich Town on 13th December 2003, aged 18.

Player Stats 2003-04					
Competition	Apps	Subs	⚽	☐	◼
League	0	1	0	0	0
Total	0	1	0	0	0

Personal Info

Position: **Striker**

Nationality: **Rep of Ireland**

Date of Birth: **27/10/1985**

Height: **5' 10" (178cm)**

Weight: **11st 4lbs (71.73kg)**

MILLWALL CLUB SHOP

Opening times
Monday - Friday   9.30am - 4.30pm
Matchday Saturdays   10am - 2.50pm and after the game unless otherwise stated
Non-Matchday Saturdays 10am - 2pm.

You can order your goods over the phone by ringing the Club Shop on **0207 231 9845.**

You can also order a selected range of items 24 hours a day, seven days a week via our online Club Shop at **www.millwallfc.co.uk.**

We accept all major credit cards over our Secure Server and we offer 128 bit encryption technology to make sure your online shopping is as safe, as it is enjoyable. If you wish to make a purchase over the internet, please read our info page first. Unfortunately, the minimum order that we can accept on credit cards is £5.

The Millwall Club Shop is situated in Bolina Road next to The Den.

Brighton & Hove Albion

Home Kit

Away Kit

Useful Information

Nickname: **The Seagulls**

Manager: **Mark McGhee**

Chairman: **Dick Knight**

Website: **www.bhafc.co.uk**

Address: **Tongdean Lane, Brighton BN1 5JD**

Telephone: **01273 695 400**

Ticket Office: **01273 776 992**

Club Shop: **01273 776 969**

Stadium: **Withdean Stadium** Capacity: **6,960**

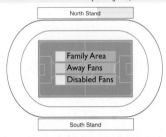

Top Goalscorer 2003-04

Leon Knight - **25 Goals**

Final Standings 2003-04

		P	W	D	L	F	A	GD	Pts
3	Bristol C	46	15	6	2	34	12	21	82
4	Brighton	46	17	4	2	39	11	21	77
5	Swindon	46	12	7	4	41	23	18	73

All-Time Record - League matches (Home and Away)

Games Played	Won	Drawn	Lost
68	27	15	26

Recent Meetings

Date	Competition	H/A	Result	Scorers
22/02/03	Division 1	A	0-1	
07/09/02	Division 1	H	1-0	Ward
05/09/00	League Cup	H	1-1	Kinet
22/08/00	League Cup	A	2-1	Braniff, Livermore
07/12/99	AW Shield	A	0-1	
05/01/99	AW Shield	A	5-1	Harris (2), Lavin, Shaw, Hockton

Player Stats

	Home	Away
Goals scored	14	11
% of team's goals: **39%**		

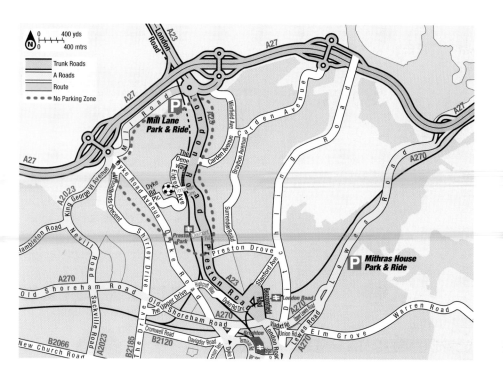

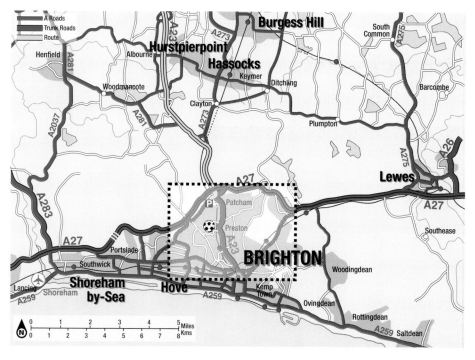

Burnley

Home Kit

Away Kit

Stadium: **Turf Moor** Capacity: **22,546**

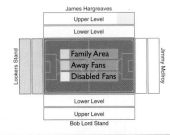

Useful Information

Nickname: **The Clarets**

Manager: **Steve Cotterill**

Chairman: **Barry Kilby**

Website: **www.burnleyfootballclub.com**

Address: **Turf Moor, Harry Potts Way**

Burnley, Lancashire BB10 4BX

Telephone: **01282 700 000**

Ticket Office: **01282 700 010**

Top Goalscorer

Robbie Blake - **19 Goals**

Final Standings 2003-04

		P	W	D	L	F	A	GD	Pts
18	Crewe	46	14	11	21	57	66	-9	53
19	Burnley	46	13	14	19	60	77	-17	53
20	Derby	46	13	13	20	53	67	-14	52

All-Time Record - League matches (Home and Away)

Games Played	Won	Drawn	Lost
46	15	15	16

Recent History

Date	Competition	H/A	Result	Scorers
28/02/04	Division 1	H	2-0	Sweeney, Ifill
14/02/04	FA Cup	H	1-0	Dichio
25/10/03	Division 1	A	1-1	Whelan
04/03/03	Division 1	H	1-1	Sadlier
17/09/02	Division 1	A	2-2	Livermore, Davies
22/12/01	Division 1	A	0-0	
25/08/01	Division 1	H	0-2	
22/04/00	Division 2	A	3-4	Harris (2), Cahill
16/10/99	Division 2	H	1-1	Cahill
23/01/99	Division 2	H	1-2	Sadlier

Player Stats

	Left Foot	Right Foot	Header
Total	3	16	0

% of team's goals: **32%**

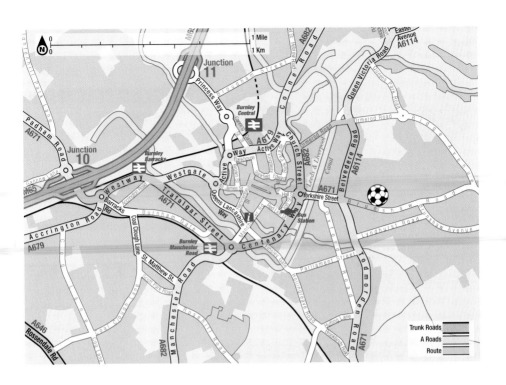

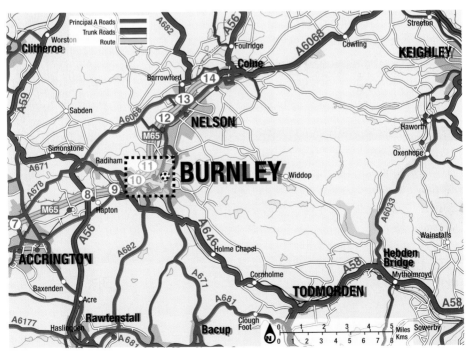

Cardiff City

Home Kit

Away Kit

Stadium: **Ninian Park** Capacity: **19,000**

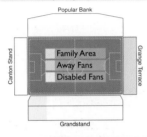

Useful Information

Nickname: **Bluebirds**

Manager: **Lennie Lawrence**

Chairman: **Sam Hammam**

Website: **www.cardiffcityfc.co.uk**

Address: **Ninian Park, Sloper Road, Cardiff CF11 8SX**

Telephone: **029 2022 1001**

Club Shop: **0845 345 1485**

Top Goalscorer 2003-04

Robert Earnshaw - **21 Goals**

Final Standings 2003-04

		P	W	D	L	F	A	GD	Pts
12	Coventry	46	17	14	15	67	54	+13	65
13	Cardiff	46	17	14	15	68	58	+10	65
14	Nottm Forest	46	15	15	16	61	58	+3	60

All-Time Record - League matches (Home and Away)

Games Played	Won	Drawn	Lost
46	16	14	16

Recent History

Date	Competition	H/A	Result	Scorers
07/04/04	Division 1	H	0-0	
20/12/03	Division 1	A	3-1	Roberts, Cahill, Sweeney
21/08/01	League Cup	H	2-1	Sadlier, Claridge
04/12/99	Division 2	H	2-0	Harris (2)
07/08/99	Division 2	A	1-1	Harris
09/12/98	AW Shield	H	2-0	Shaw, Harris
09/12/97	AW Shield	A	2-0	Shaw, Grant

Player Stats

	Left Foot	Right Foot	Header
Total	5	15	1

% of team's goals: **31%**

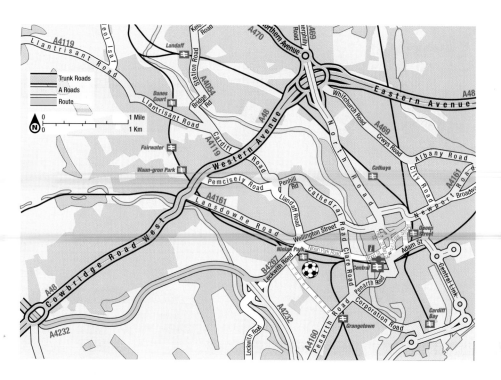

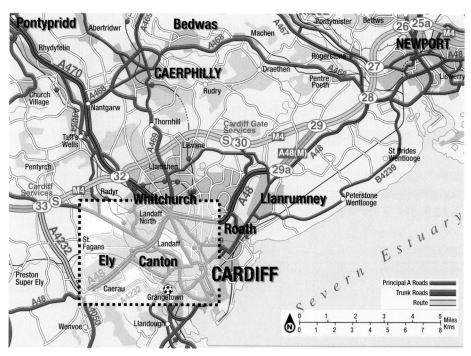

Coventry City

Home Kit

Away Kit

Stadium: **Highfield Road** Capacity: **23,633**

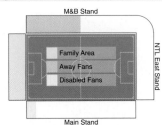

M&B Stand

Family Area
Away Fans
Disabled Fans

NTL East Stand

Main Stand

Top Goalscorer 2003-04

Gary McSheffrey - **11 Goals**

Final Standings 2003-04

	P	W	D	L	F	A	GD	Pts
11 Stoke City	46	18	12	16	58	55	+3	66
12 Coventry	46	17	14	15	67	54	+13	65
13 Cardiff	46	17	14	15	68	58	+10	65

All-Time Record - League matches (Home and Away)

Games Played	Won	Drawn	Lost
44	20	7	17

Recent History

Date	Competition	H/A	Result	Scorers
10/04/04	Division 1	A	0-4	
04/10/03	Division 1	H	2-1	Harris, Ifill
04/05/03	Division 1	H	2-0	Cahill, Craig
28/09/02	Division 1	A	3-2	Harris, Kinet, Davies
12/04/02	Division 1	A	1-0	Claridge
03/11/01	Division 1	H	3-2	Sadlier, Kinet, Claridge

Player Stats

	Left Foot	Right Foot	Header
Total	3	6	2
% of team's goals:	16%		

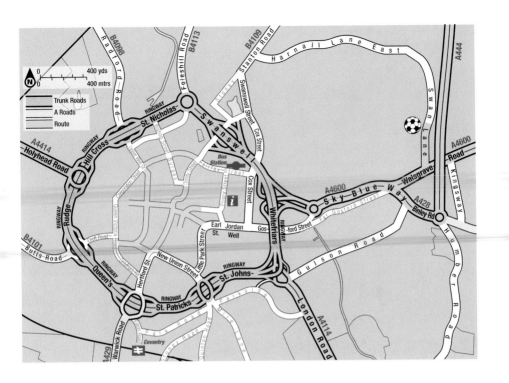

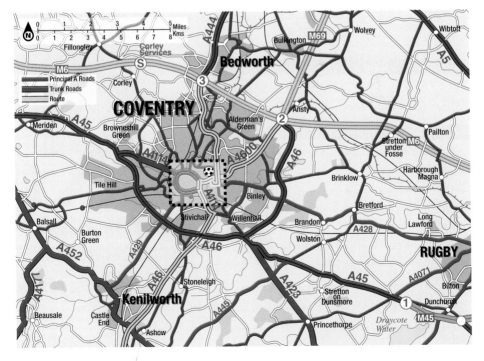

Crewe Alexandra

Home Kit

Away Kit

Stadium: **The Alexandra Stadium** Capacity: **10,046**

Railwaytrack Stand

Family Stand

Family Area
Away Fans
Disabled Fans

Gresty Stand

Ringsway Stand

Top Goalscorer 2003-04

Dean Ashton - **19 Goals**

Final Standings 2003-04

	P	W	D	L	F	A	GD	Pts
17 Rotherham	46	13	15	18	53	61	-8	54
18 Crewe	46	14	11	21	57	66	-9	53
19 Burnley	46	13	14	19	60	77	-17	53

All-Time Record - League matches (Home and Away)

Games Played	Won	Drawn	Lost
18	6	5	7

Recent History

Date	Competition	H/A	Result	Scorers
31/01/04	Division 1	A	2-1	Dichio (2)
23/08/03	Division 1	H	1-1	Whelan
29/12/01	Division 1	H	2-0	Reid, Cahill
28/08/01	Division 1	A	0-1	
18/03/97	Division 2	A	0-0	
21/09/96	Division 2	H	2-0	Huckerby, Dair

Player Stats

	Left Foot	Right Foot	Header
Total	6	9	4
% of team's goals:	**33%**		

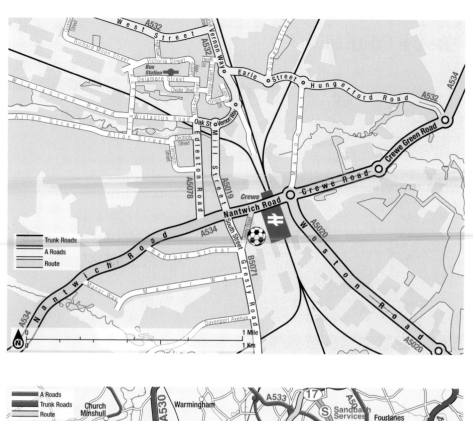

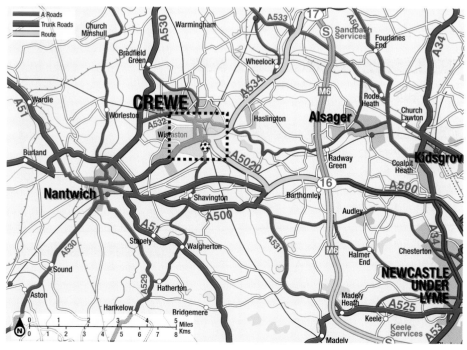

Derby County

Home Kit

Away Kit

Stadium: **Pride Park** Capacity: **33,597**

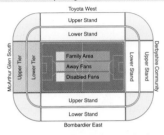

Top Goalscorer 2003-04

Ian Taylor - **11 Goals**

Final Standings 2003-04

		P	W	D	L	F	A	GD	Pts
19	Burnley	46	13	14	19	60	77	-17	53
20	Derby	46	13	13	20	53	67	-14	52
21	Gillingham	46	14	9	23	48	67	-19	51

All-Time Record - League matches (Home and Away)

Games Played	Won	Drawn	Lost
28	11	8	9

Recent History

Date	Competition	H/A	Result	Scorers
01/05/04	Division 1	A	0-2	
22/11/03	Division 1	H	0-0	
16/04/03	Division 1	A	2-1	Harris, McCammon
26/10/02	Division 1	H	3-0	Wise, Harris (2)
16/12/95	Division 1	H	0-1	
01/10/95	Division 1	A	2-2	Black, Rae
11/03/95	Division 1	A	2-3	Rae, Mitchell
27/08/94	Division 1	H	4-1	Rae, Kerr (3)
18/05/94	Play-Off	H	1-3	Berry
15/05/94	Play-Off	A	0-2	

Player Stats

	Left Foot	Right Foot	Header
Total	9	2	-
% of team's goals	21%		

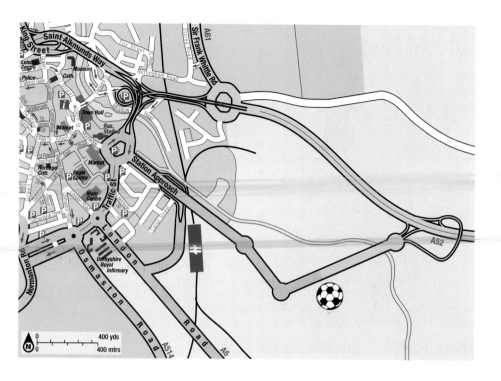

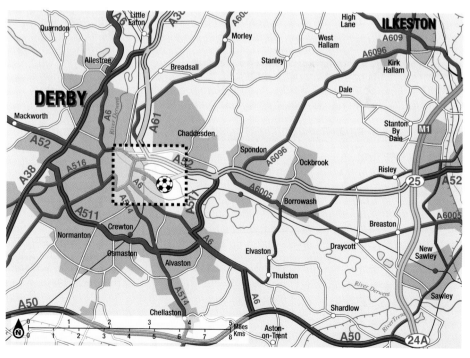

Gillingham

Home Kit

Away Kit

Stadium: **Priestfield Stadium** Capacity: **10,952**

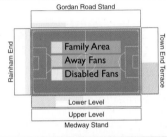

Useful Information

Nickname: **The Gills**

Manager: **Andy Hessenthaler**

Chairman: **Paul Scally**

Website: **www.gillinghamfootballclub.com**

Address: **Priestfield Stadium,**

Redfern Avenue, Gillingham,

Kent ME7 4DD

Telephone: **01634 300 000**

Ticket Office: **01634 851 854**

Top Goalscorer 2003-04

Daniel Spiller - 6 Goals

Final Standings 2003-04

		P	W	D	L	F	A	GD	Pts
20	Derby	46	13	13	20	53	67	-14	52
21	Gillingham	46	14	9	23	48	67	-19	51
22	Walsall	46	13	12	21	45	65	-20	51

All-Time Record - League matches (Home and Away)

Games Played	Won	Drawn	Lost
78	39	17	22

Recent History

Date	Competition	H/A	Result	Scorers
28/12/03	Division 1	H	1-2	Chadwick
06/09/03	Division 1	A	3-4	Ifill, Peeters (2)
26/12/02	Division 1	H	2-2	Ryan, Harris
17/08/02	Division 1	A	0-1	
24/03/02	Division 1	H	0-1	
24/11/01	Division 1	H	1-2	Cahill
12/09/01	League Cup	A	1-2	Moody
24/04/00	Division 2	H	2-2	Moody, Ifill
02/10/99	Division 2	A	0-2	
16/02/99	AW Shield	H	1-0	Sadlier

Player Stats

	Left Foot	Right Foot	Header
D.Spiller	-	3	3
P.Shaw	1	4	1
P.Agyemang	1	3	2

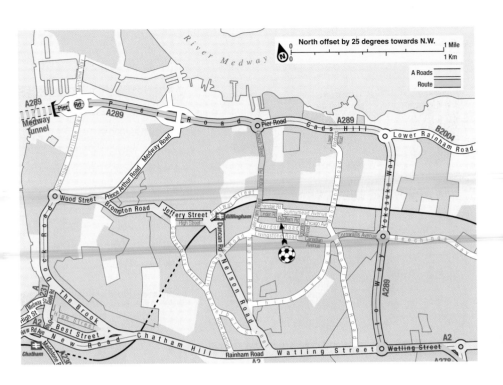

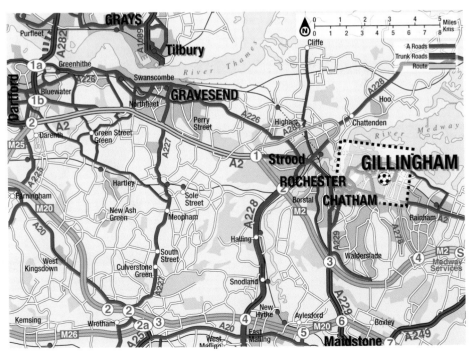

Ipswich Town

Home Kit

Away Kit

Stadium: **Portman Road** Capacity: **30,300**

Useful Information

Nickname: **Blues, Town, Tractor Boys**

Manager: **Joe Royle**

Chairman: **David Sheepshanks**

Website: **www.itfc.co.uk**

Address: **Portman Road,**

Ipswich, IP1 2DA

Telephone: **01473 400 500**

Ticket Office: **0845 605 0129**

Club Shop: **01473 400 501**

Top Goalscorer 2003-04

Darren Bent - 16 Goals

Final Standings 2003-04

		P	W	D	L	F	A	GD	Pts
4	West Ham	46	19	17	10	67	45	22	74
5	Ipswich	46	21	10	15	84	72	12	73
6	C Palace	46	21	10	15	72	61	11	73

All-Time Record - League matches (Home and Away)

Games Played	Won	Drawn	Lost
34	13	11	10

Recent History

Date	Competition	H/A	Result	Scorers
13/03/04	Division 1	A	3-1	Harris (2), Ward
13/12/03	Division 1	H	0-0	
01/01/03	Division 1	A	1-4	Reid
24/08/02	Division 1	H	1-1	May
26/09/00	League Cup	A	0-5	
19/09/00	League Cup	H	2-0	Cahill, Ifill
05/05/96	Division 1	A	0-0	
11/11/95	Division 1	H	2-1	Witter, Malkin

Player Stats

	Left Foot	Right Foot	Header
Total	4	9	3
% of team's goals:	19%		

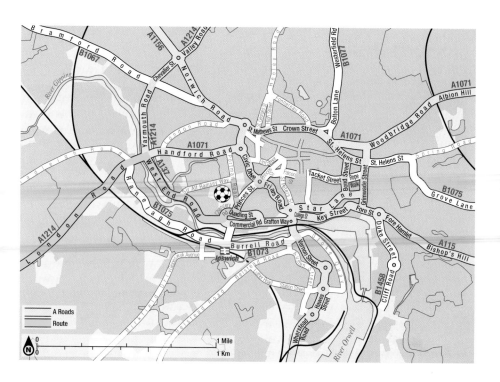

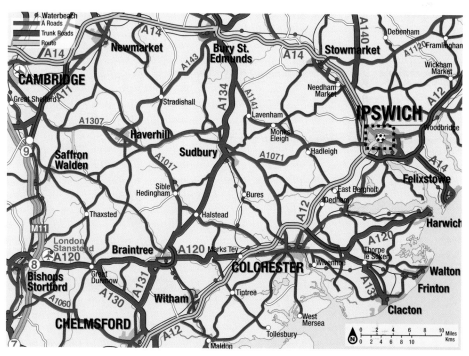

Leeds United

Home Kit

Away Kit

Stadium: **Elland Road** Capacity: **40,204**

East Stand (Upper Tier)
Executive Boxes
East Stand (Lower Tier)
Family Area
Away Fans either
South East corner
or South Stand
Disabled Fans
West Stand (Lower Tier)
West Stand (Upper Tier)

Useful Information

Nickname: **United**

Manager: **Kevin Blackwell**

Chairman: **Gerald Krasner**

Website: **www.lufc.com**

Address: **Elland Road,**

Leeds LS11 0ES

Telephone: **0113 226 6000**

Fax: **0113 367 6050**

Ticket Office: **0845 121 1992**

Top Goalscorer 2003-04

Mark Viduka - **11 Goals**

Final Standings 2003-04

		P	W	D	L	F	A	GD	Pts
18	Leicester	38	6	15	17	48	65	-17	33
19	Leeds	38	8	9	21	40	79	-39	33
20	Wolves	38	7	12	19	38	77	-39	33

All-Time Record - League matches (Home and Away)

Games Played	Won	Drawn	Lost
10	4	1	5

Recent History

Date	Competition	H/A	Result	Scorers
06/04/88	Division 2	A	2-1	Walker, Sheringham
14/11/87	Division 2	H	3-1	Cascarino (3)
04/04/87	Division 2	A	0-2	
08/11/86	Division 2	H	1-0	Sheringham
12/04/86	Division 2	A	1-3	Wilson
09/11/85	Division 2	H	3-1	Lovell, Lowndes, Baird (og)

Player Stats

	Left Foot	Right Foot	Header
Total	3	8	-
% of team's goals	28%		

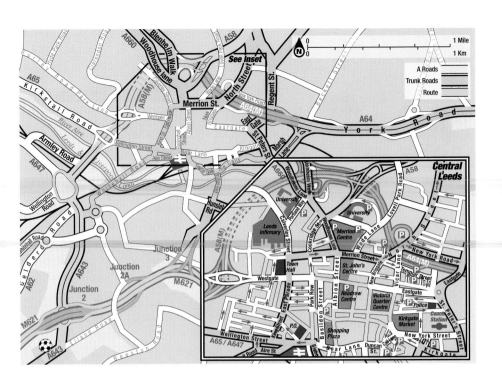

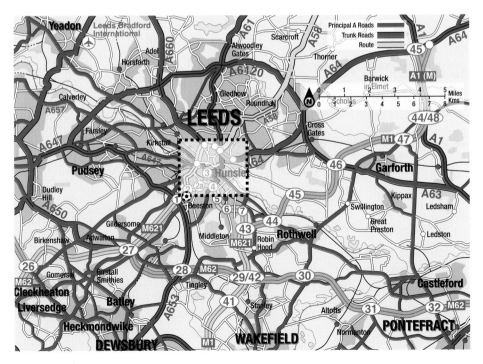

Leicester City

Home Kit

Away Kit

Stadium: **Walkers Stadium** Capacity: **32,500**

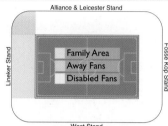

Useful Information

Nickname: **The Foxes**

Manager: **Micky Adams**

Chairman: **Jim McCahill**

Website: **www.lcfc.co.uk**

Address: **The Walkers Stadium**

Filbert Way, Leicester LE2 7FL

Telephone: **0870 040 6000**

Top Goalscorer 2003-04

Les Ferdinand - **12 Goals**

Final Standings 2003-04

		P	W	D	L	F	A	GD	Pts
17	Everton	38	9	12	17	45	57	-12	39
18	Leicester	38	6	15	17	48	65	-17	33
19	Leeds	38	8	9	21	40	79	-39	33

All-Time Record - League matches (Home and Away)

Games Played	Won	Drawn	Lost
24	10	7	7

Recent History

Date	Competition	H/A	Result	Scorers
14/12/02	Division 1	A	1-4	Claridge
16/11/02	Division 1	H	2-2	Reid, Wise
23/03/96	Division 1	A	1-2	Rae
01/01/96	Division 1	H	1-1	Malkin
28/08/93	Division 1	A	0-4	
14/04/93	Division 1	A	0-3	
28/12/92	Division 1	H	2-0	Moralee, Goodman

Player Stats

	Left Foot	Right Foot	Header
Total	-	5	7

% of team's goals: **25%**

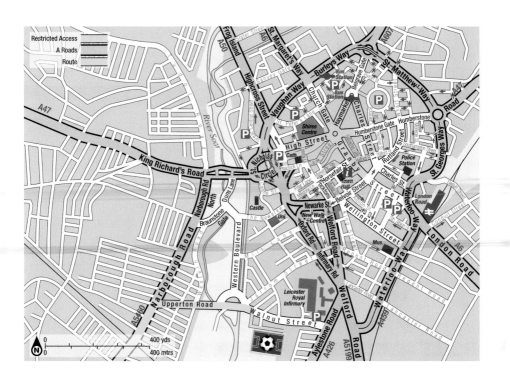

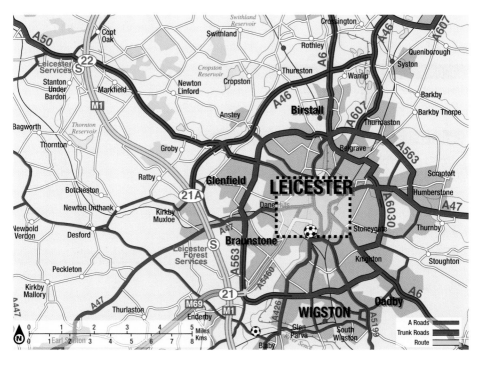

Nottingham Forest

Home Kit

Away Kit

Stadium: **City Ground** Capacity: **30,602**

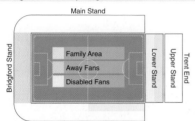

Useful Information

Nickname: **Reds**

Manager: **Joe Kinnear**

Chairman: **Nigel Doughty**

Website: **www.nottinghamforest.co.uk**

Address: **City Ground,**

Nottingham NG2 5FJ

Telephone: **0115 982 4444**

Ticket Office: **0115 982 4445**

Top Goalscorer 2003-04

Andy Reid - **13 Goals**

Final Standings 2003-04

		P	W	D	L	F	A	GD	Pts
13	Cardiff	46	17	14	15	68	58	+10	65
14	Nottm Forest	46	15	15	16	61	58	+3	60
15	Preston	46	15	14	17	69	71	-2	59

All-Time Record - League matches (Home and Away)

Games Played	Won	Drawn	Lost
42	14	14	14

Recent History

Date	Competition	H/A	Result	Scorers
17/04/04	Division 1	A	2-2	Livermore, Chadwick
01/11/03	Division 1	H	1-0	Braniff
26/04/03	Division 1	A	3-3	Nethercott, Cahill, Harris
05/10/02	Division 1	H	1-2	Davies
09/02/02	Division 1	A	2-1	Ifill, Cahill
20/10/01	Division 1	H	3-3	Cahill, Ifill, Sadlier
30/11/94	League Cup	H	2-0	Berry (2)
17/04/94	Division 1	H	2-2	Moralee, Mitchell
03/11/93	Division 1	A	3-1	Goodman, Murray, Stevens

Player Stats

	Left Foot	Right Foot	Header
Total	10	2	1
% of team's goals:	21%		

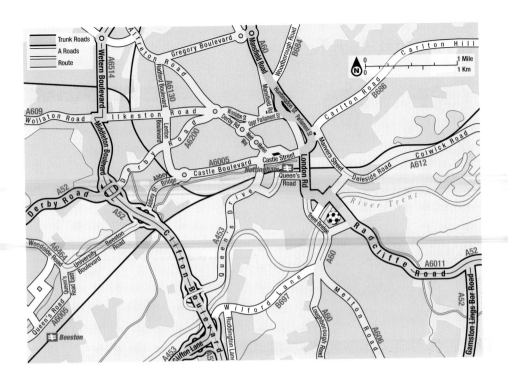

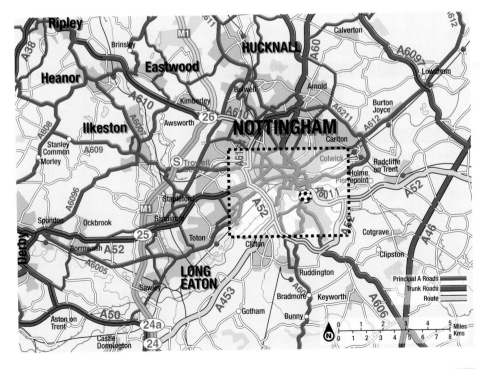

Plymouth Argyle

Home Kit

Away Kit

Stadium: **Home Park** Capacity: **19,630**

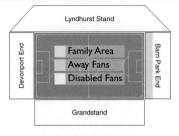

Useful Information

Nickname: **The Pilgrims**

Manager: **Bobby Williamson**

Chairman: **Paul Stapleton**

Website: **www.pafc.co.uk**

Address: **Home Park, Plymouth, Devon PL2 3DQ**

Telephone: **01752 562 561**

Top Goalscorer 2003-04

David Friio - **14 Goals**

Final Standings 2003-04

		P	W	D	L	F	A	GD	Pts
1	Plymouth	46	17	5	1	52	13	+44	90
2	QPR	46	16	7	0	47	12	+35	83
3	Bristol C	46	15	6	2	34	12	+21	82

All-Time Record - League matches (Home and Away)

Games Played	Won	Drawn	Lost
68	20	24	24

Recent History

Date	Competition	H/A	Result	Scorers
13/04/98	Division 2	H	1-1	Hockton
13/12/97	Division 2	A	0-3	
12/04/97	Division 2	H	0-0	
05/10/96	Division 2	A	0-0	

Player Stats

	Home	Away
Goals scored	8	6
% of team's goals: **27%**		

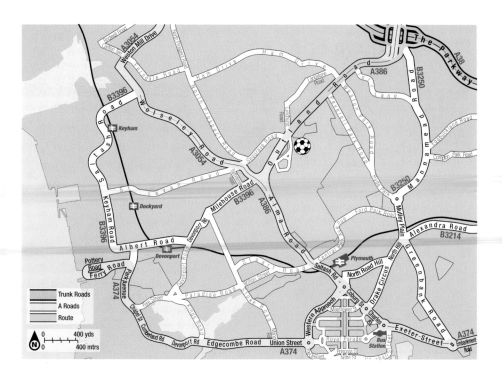

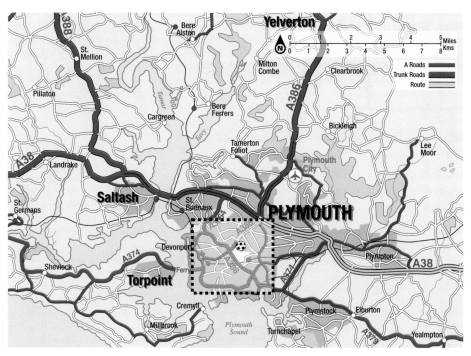

Preston North End

PRESTON NORTH END FC

Home Kit

Away Kit

Stadium: **Deepdale** Capacity: **21,412**

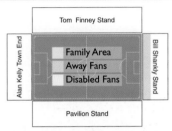

Tom Finney Stand

Alan Kelly Town End

Family Area
Away Fans
Disabled Fans

Bill Shankly Stand

Pavilion Stand

Useful Information

Nickname: **The Lilywhites, North End**

Manager: **Craig Brown**

Chairman: **Derek Shaw**

Website: **www.pnefc.net**

Address: **Deepdale, Sir Tom Finney Way, Preston PR1 6RU**

Telephone: **01772 902 020**

Ticket Office: **01772 902 222**

Top Goalscorer 2003-04

Ricardo Fuller - **17 Goals**

Final Standings 2003-04

		P	W	D	L	F	A	GD	Pts
14	Nottm Forest	46	15	15	16	61	58	+3	60
15	Preston	46	15	14	17	69	71	-2	59
16	Watford	46	15	12	19	54	68	-14	57

All-Time Record - League matches (Home and Away)

Games Played	Won	Drawn	Lost
51	24	7	20

Recent History

Date	Competition	H/A	Result	Scorers
21/02/04	Division 1	A	2-1	Ifill, Cahill
14/10/03	Division 1	H	0-1	
08/02/03	Division 1	A	1-2	Kinet
09/11/02	Division 1	H	2-1	Ifill, Wise
05/03/02	Division 1	H	2-1	Claridge (2)
15/09/01	Division 1	A	0-1	

Player Stats

	Left Foot	Right Foot	Header
Total	5	7	5
% of team's goals:	25%		

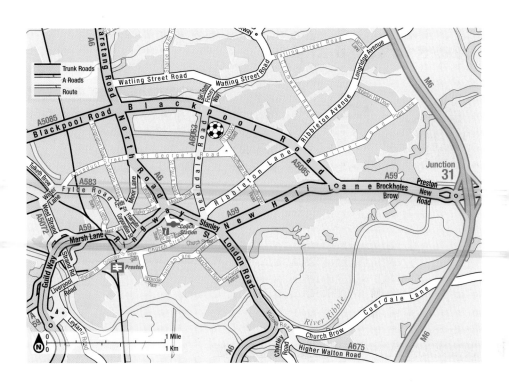

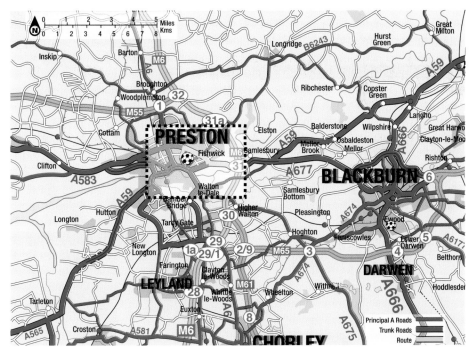

Queens Park Rangers

Home Kit

Away Kit

Stadium: **Loftus Road** Capacity: **19,142**

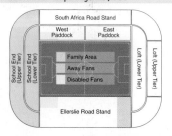

Useful Information

Nickname: **Rs, Rangers**

Manager: **Ian Holloway**

Chairman: **Bill Power**

Website: **www.qpr.co.uk**

Address: **South Africa Road,**

London, W12 7PA

Telephone: **020 8743 0262**

Top Goalscorer 2003-04

Kevin Gallen - **17 Goals**

Final Standings 2003-04

		P	W	D	L	F	A	GD	Pts
1	Plymouth	46	17	5	1	52	13	44	90
2	QPR	46	16	7	0	47	12	35	83
3	Bristol C	46	15	6	2	34	12	21	82

All-Time Record - League matches (Home and Away)

Games Played	Won	Drawn	Lost
56	27	14	15

Recent History

Date	Competition	H/A	Result	Scorers
18/02/95	FA Cup	A	0-1	
27/10/93	League Cup	A	0-3	

Player Stats

	Home	Away
Goals scored	**12**	**5**
% of team's goals:	**36%**	

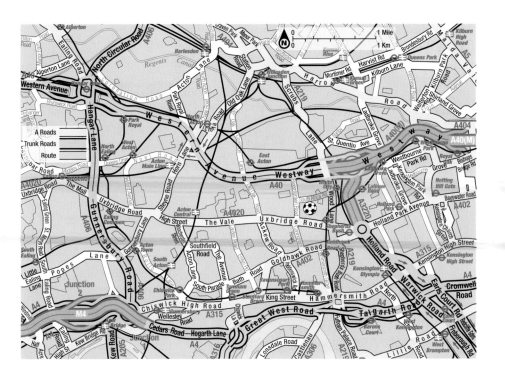

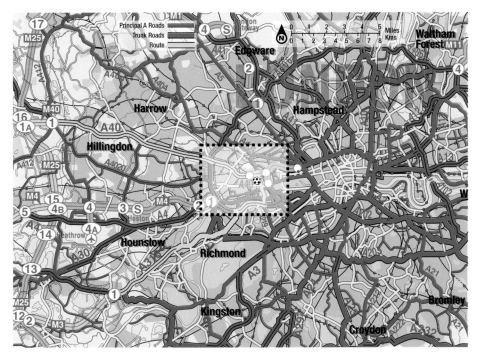

Reading

Home Kit

Away Kit

Stadium: **Madejski Stadium** Capacity: **24,200**

Kit@ West Stand

Foster's South Stand

npower North Stand

Family Area
Away Fans
Disabled Fans

Kyocera Mita East Stand

Top Goalscorer 2003-04

Shaun Goater - **12 Goals**

Final Standings 2003-04

		P	W	D	L	F	A	GD	Pts
8	Sheff Utd	46	11	6	6	37	25	9	71
9	Reading	46	11	6	6	29	25	-2	70
10	Millwall	46	11	8	4	28	15	7	69

All-Time Record - League matches (Home and Away)

Games Played	Won	Drawn	Lost
80	32	17	31

Recent History

Date	Competition	H/A	Result	Scorers
24/04/04	Division 1	H	0-1	
15/11/03	Division 1	A	0-1	
15/02/03	Division 1	H	0-2	
02/11/02	Division 1	A	2-0	
06/01/01	Division 2	A	4-3	Harris (3), Newman(og)
12/08/00	Division 2	H	2-0	Cahill (2)
12/02/00	Division 2	A	0-2	
16/11/99	Division 2	H	5-0	Moody (3), Harris (2)
01/05/99	Division 2	A	0-2	
12/12/98	Division 2	H	1-1	Neill

Player Stats

	Left Foot	Right Foot	Header
Total	4	7	1

% of team's goals: **22%**

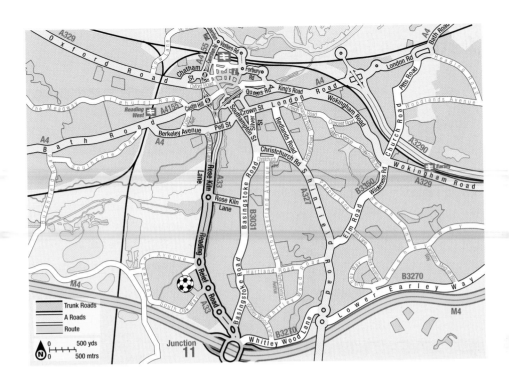

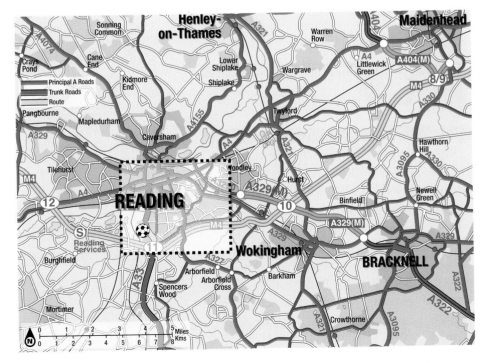

Rotherham United

Home Kit

Away Kit

Stadium: **Millmoor** Capacity: **11,514**

Top Goalscorer 2003-04

Martin Butler - **15 Goals**

Final Standings 2003-04

		P	W	D	L	F	A	GD	Pts
16	Watford	46	9	8	6	31	28	-14	57
17	Rotherham	46	8	8	7	31	27	-8	54
18	Crewe	46	11	3	9	33	26	-9	53

All-Time Record - League matches (Home and Away)

Games Played	Won	Drawn	Lost
24	9	7	8

Recent History

Date	Competition	H/A	Result	Scorers
24/02/04	Division 1	H	2-1	Harris, Cahill
11/10/03	Division 1	A	0-0	
28/12/02	Division 1	A	3-1	Harris, Reid, Claridge
10/08/02	Division 1	H	0-6	
01/04/02	Division 1	A	0-0	
09/11/01	Division 1	H	1-0	Cahill
07/04/01	Division 2	H	4-0	Cahill, Reid, Claridge (2)
02/12/00	Division 2	A	2-3	Reid (2)
15/02/97	Division 2	H	2-0	Crawford, Gayle (og)
23/11/96	Division 2	A	0-0	

Player Stats

	Left Foot	Right Foot	Header
Total	6	5	4

% of team's goals: **28%**

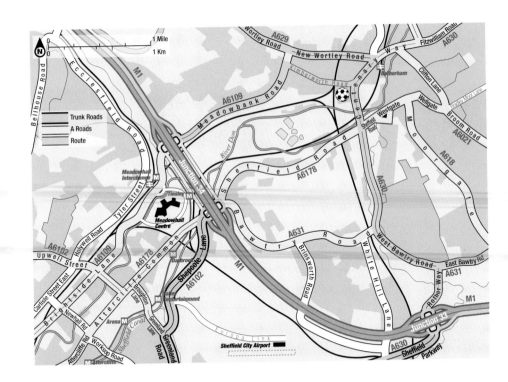

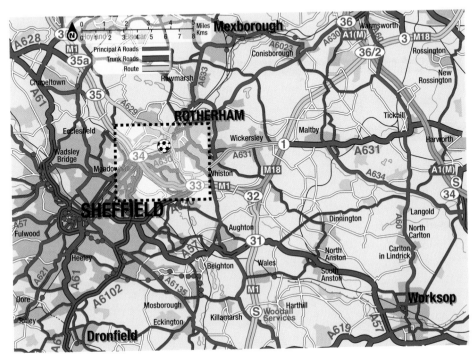

Sheffield United

Home Kit | Away Kit

Useful Information

Nickname: **The Blades**

Manager: **Neil Warnock**

Chairman: **Derek Dooley MBE**

Website: **www.sufc.co.uk**

Address: **Bramall Lane,**

Sheffield S2 4SU

Telephone: **0114 221 5757**

Box Office: **0114 221 3132**

Club Shop: **0114 221 3132**

Stadium: **Bramall Lane** Capacity: **30,413**

The Arnold Laver Stand

The Hallam FM Kop

Family Area
Away Fans
Disabled Fans

Bramall Lane

The DeSun Stand

Top Goalscorer 2003-04

Jack Lester - **12 Goals**

Final Standings 2003-04

		P	W	D	L	F	A	GD	Pts
7	Wigan	46	11	8	4	29	16	15	71
8	Sheff Utd	46	11	6	6	37	25	9	71
9	Reading	46	11	6	6	29	25	-2	70

All-Time Record - League matches (Home and Away)

Games Played	Won	Drawn	Lost
38	16	6	16

Recent History

Date	Competition	H/A	Result	Scorers
02/03/04	Division 1	A	1-2	Ifill
18/10/03	Division 1	H	2-0	Harris, Ifill
01/02/03	Division 1	H	1-0	Ifill
27/08/02	Division 1	A	1-3	Ifill
19/03/02	Division 1	A	2-3	Ifill, Nethercott
22/09/01	Division 1	H	2-0	Nethercott, Kinet
16/03/96	Division 1	H	1-0	Fuchs
13/02/96	Division 1	A	0-2	
14/01/95	Division 1	A	1-1	Beard
29/10/94	Division 1	H	3-1	Cadette, Kennedy

Player Stats

	Left Foot	Right Foot	Header
Total	1	10	1
% of team's goals: **18%**			

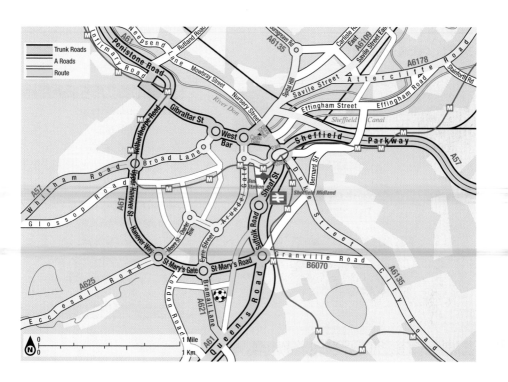

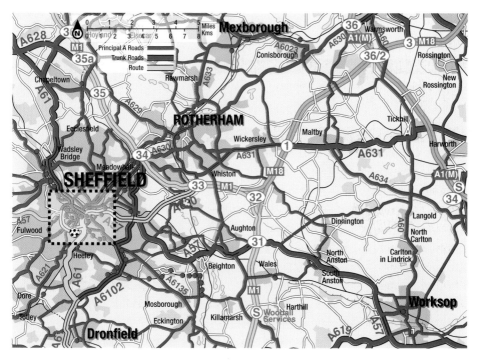

Stoke City

Home Kit

Away Kit

Stadium: **Britannia Stadium** Capacity: **28,384**

The John Smith's Stand
Upper Tier
Lower Tier
The Big Stand
Family Area
Away Fans
Disabled Fans
The Genesis Boothen End
The Sentinel Stand

Useful Information

Nickname: **The Potters**

Manager: **Tony Pulis**

Chairman: **Gunnar Gislason**

Website: **www.stokecityfc.com**

Address: **Britannia Stadium, Stanley Matthews Way, Stoke-on-Trent, Staffordshire ST4 4EG**

Telephone: **01782 592 222**

Ticket Office: **01782 592 200**

Club Shop: **01782 592 244**

Joint Top Goalscorer 2003-04

Gifton Noel-Williams
-10 Goals

Final Standings 2003-04

		P	W	D	L	F	A	GD	Pts
10	Millwall	46	11	8	4	28	15	7	69
11	Stoke	46	11	7	5	35	24	3	66
12	Coventry	46	9	9	5	34	22	13	65

All-Time Record - League matches (Home and Away)

Games Played	Won	Drawn	Lost
36	14	9	13

Recent History

Date	Competition	H/A	Result	Scorers
07/02/04	Division 1	H	1-1	Dichio
26/08/03	Division 1	A	0-0	
12/04/03	Division 1	H	3-1	Harris, Roberts, Livermore
23/11/02	Division 1	A	1-0	Reid
03/04/01	Division 2	H	2-0	Sadlier, Cahill
21/10/00	Division 2	A	2-3	Harris (2)
22/01/00	Division 2	H	1-0	Gilkes
22/08/99	Division 2	A	1-3	Bircham
20/02/99	Division 2	H	2-0	Harris, Cahill
12/09/98	Division 2	A	0-1	

Player Stats

	Left Foot	Right Foot	Header
G.N-Williams	1	5	4
A.Akinbiyi	2	7	1

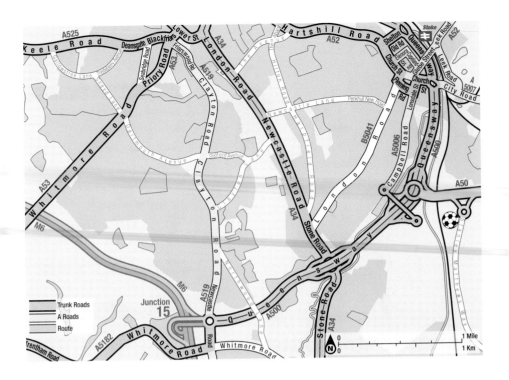

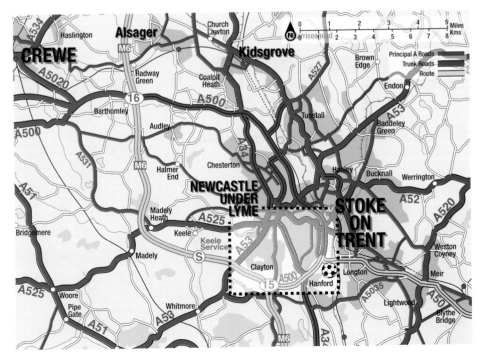

Sunderland

Home Kit

Away Kit

Stadium: **Stadium of Light** Capacity: **48,300**

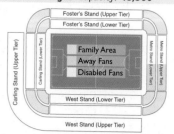

Top Goalscorer 2003-04

Marcus Stewart - **14 Goals**

Final Standings 2003-04

		P	W	D	L	F	A	GD	Pts
2	West Brom	46	14	5	4	34	16	22	86
3	Sunderland	46	13	8	2	33	15	17	79
4	West Ham	46	12	7	4	42	20	22	74

All-Time Record - League matches (Home and Away)

Games Played	Won	Drawn	Lost
30	10	7	13

Recent History

Date	Competition	H/A	Result	Scorers
04/04/04	FA Cup	A	1-0	Cahill
17/01/04	Division 1	H	2-1	Dichio (2)
16/08/03	Division 1	A	1-0	Whelan
09/12/95	Division 1	A	0-6	
23/09/95	Division 1	H	1-2	Scott, Smith
10/12/94	Division 1	H	2-0	Kennedy, Mitchell
04/10/94	League Cup	A	1-1	Goodman
21/09/94	League Cup	H	2-1	Goodman, Kennedy
20/08/94	Division 1	A	1-1	Rae

Player Stats

	Left Foot	Right Foot	Header
Total	9	2	3

% of team's goals: **23%**

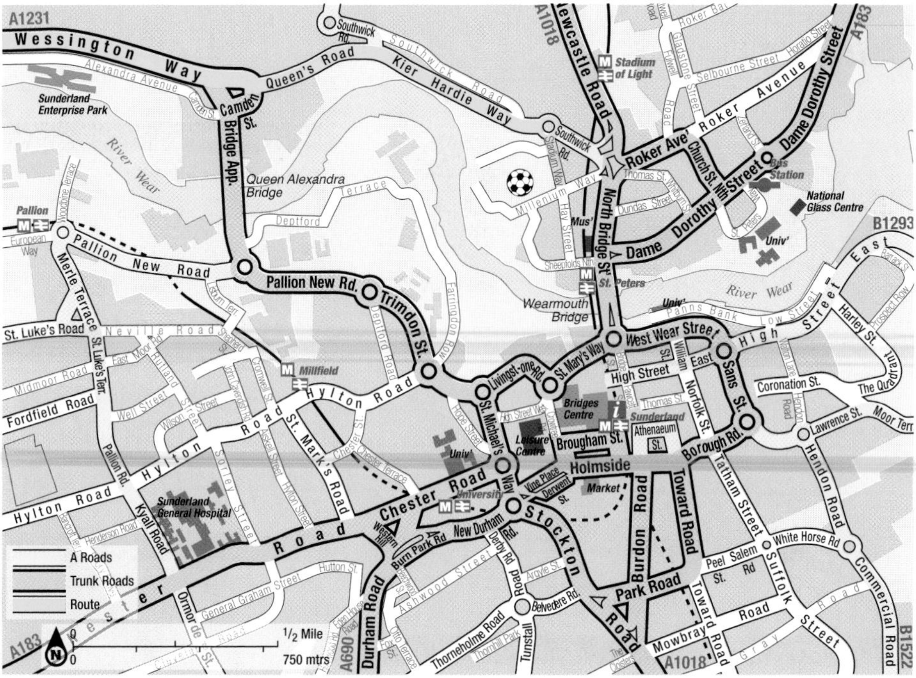
Wessington Way
Queen's Road
Kier Hardie Way
Sunderland Enterprise Park
Camden St.
Bridge App.
River Wear
Queen Alexandra Bridge
Pallion
Pallion New Road
Pallion New Rd.
Trimdon St.
Newcastle Road
Stadium of Light
Roker Avenue
Dame Dorothy Street
North Bridge St.
Bus Station
National Glass Centre
Univ'
St. Peters
Wearmouth Bridge
West Wear Street
High Street
Millfield
Hylton Road
St. Michael's Way
Bridges Centre
Sunderland
Leisure Centre
Brougham St.
Holmside
Market
University
Chester Road
Stockton Road
Sunderland General Hospital
Burdon Road
Toward Road
Park Road
Borough Rd.
Sans St.
Hendon Road
Suffolk Street
Commercial Road
Durham Road
Tunstall Road
Mowbray Road
A Roads
Trunk Roads
Route
1/2 Mile
750 mtrs

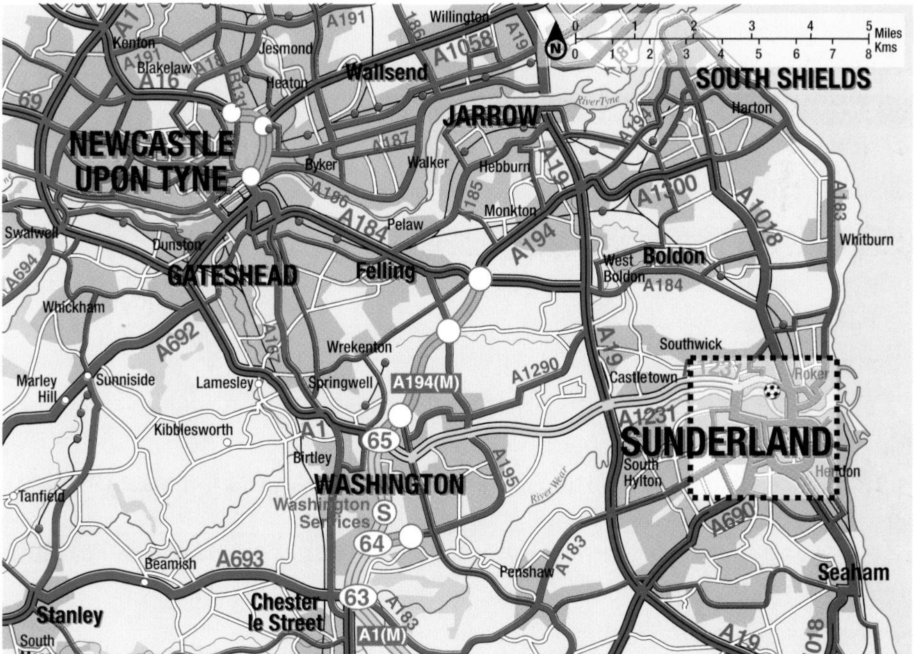
NEWCASTLE UPON TYNE
GATESHEAD
Wallsend
JARROW
SOUTH SHIELDS
Felling
Boldon
WASHINGTON
SUNDERLAND
Chester le Street
Stanley
Seaham
Whitburn
Southwick
Castletown
A1(M)
A194(M)
Miles
Kms

Watford

Home Kit

Away Kit

Stadium: Vicarage Road Capacity: **22,000**

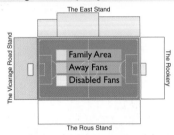

The East Stand

The Vicarage Road Stand

Family Area
Away Fans
Disabled Fans

The Rookery

The Rous Stand

Top Goalscorer 2003-04

Scott Fitzgerald - **10 Goals**

Final Standings 2003-04

		P	W	D	L	F	A	GD	Pts
15	Preston	46	11	7	5	43	29	-2	59
16	Watford	46	9	8	6	31	28	-14	57
17	Rotherham	46	8	8	7	31	27	-8	54

All-Time Record - League matches (Home and Away)

Games Played	Won	Drawn	Lost
82	38	23	21

Recent History

Date	Competition	H/A	Result	Scorers
20/04/04	Division 1	H	2-1	Dichio
13/09/03	Division 1	A	1-3	Ifill
11/01/03	Division 1	H	4-0	Claridge, Ryan, Ifill, Sweeney
13/08/02	Division 1	A	0-0	
15/01/02	Division 1	H	1-0	Claridge
01/01/02	Division 1	A	4-1	Cahill, Sadlier, Reid, Harris
25/02/98	Division 2	H	1-1	Shaw
18/10/97	Division 2	A	1-0	Shaw
22/03/97	Division 2	H	0-1	
24/08/96	Division 2	A	2-0	Harle, Crawford

Player Stats

	Left Foot	Right Foot	Header
Total	1	6	3

% of team's goals: **19%**

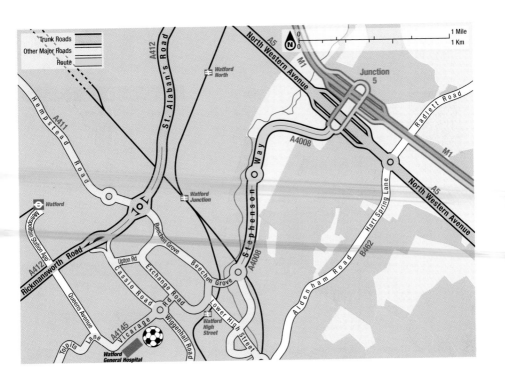

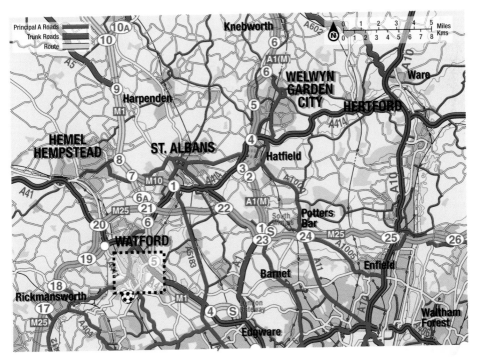

West Ham United

Home Kit

Away Kit

Stadium: Upton Park Capacity: **35,500**

Useful Information

Nickname: **The Hammers**

Manager: **Alan Pardew**

Chairman: **Terry Brown**

Website: **www.whufc.co.uk**

Address: **Upton Park, Green Street, London E13 9AZ**

Telephone: **020 8548 2748**

Ticket Office: **020 8548 2700**

Top Goalscorer 2003-04

Marlon Harewood - **13 Goals**

Final Standings 2003-04

		P	W	D	L	F	A	GD	Pts
3	Sunderland	46	13	8	2	33	15	17	79
4	West Ham	46	12	7	4	42	20	22	74
5	Ipswich Town	46	12	3	8	49	36	12	73

All-Time Record - League matches (Home and Away)

Games Played	Won	Drawn	Lost
20	4	9	7

Recent History

Date	Competition	H/A	Result	Scorers
21/03/04	Division 1	H	4-1	Cahill (2), Dailly (og), Chadwick
28/09/03	Division 1	A	1-1	Cahill
28/03/93	Division 1	A	2-2	Moralee, Stevens
15/11/92	Division 1	H	2-1	Allen, Barber

Player Stats

	Left Foot	Right Foot	Header
Total	-	11	2

% of team's goals: **19%**

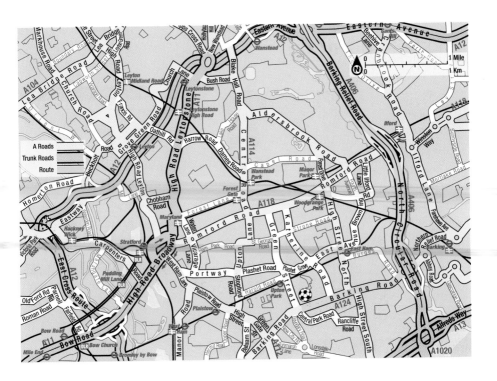

A Roads
Trunk Roads
Route

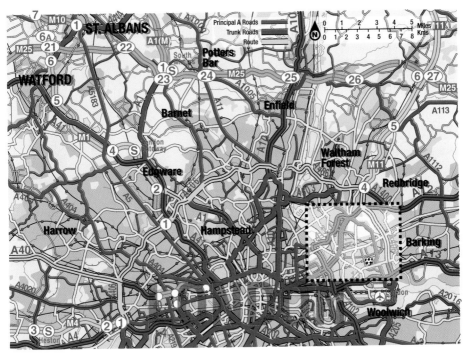

Principal A Roads
Trunk Roads
Route

Wigan Athletic

Home Kit

Away Kit

Stadium: **JJB Stadium** Capacity: **25,000**

Useful Information

Nickname: **The Latics**

Manager: **Paul Jewell**

Chairman: **David Whelan**

Website: **www.wiganlatics.co.uk**

Address: **JJB Stadium, Robin Park, Newtown, Wigan WN5 0UZ**

Telephone: **01942 774 000**

Ticket Office: **01942 770410**

Top Goalscorer 2003-04

Nathan Ellington - **18 Goals**

Final Standings 2003-04

		P	W	D	L	F	A	GD	Pts
6	C Palace	46	10	8	5	34	25	11	73
7	Wigan	46	11	8	4	29	16	15	71
8	Sheff Utd	46	11	6	6	37	25	9	71

All-Time Record - League matches (Home and Away)

Games Played	Won	Drawn	Lost
16	8	6	2

Recent History

Date	Competition	H/A	Result	Scorers
10/01/04	Division 1	A	0-0	
09/08/03	Division 2	H	2-0	Wise, Cahill
13/01/01	Division 2	H	3-1	Moody (3)
07/11/00	Division 2	A	0-1	
17/05/00	Play-Off	A	0-1	
13/05/00	Play-Off	H	0-0	
15/01/00	Division 2	A	1-1	Livermore
14/08/99	Division 2	H	3-3	Shaw, Cahill, Harris

Player Stats

	Left Foot	Right Foot	Header
Total	4	8	6

% of team's goals: **30%**

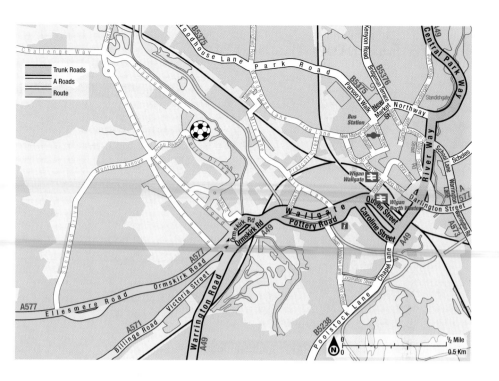

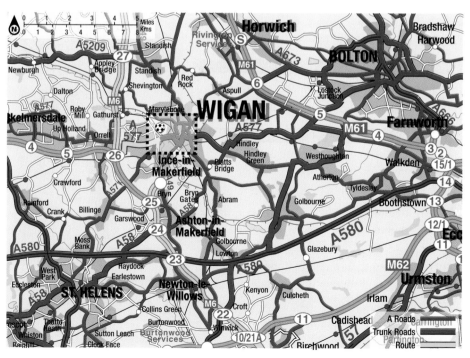

Wolverhampton Wanderers

Home Kit

Away Kit

Stadium: Molineux Stadium Capacity: **28,525**

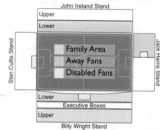

Useful Information

Nickname: **Wolves**

Manager: **Dave Jones**

Chairman: **Rick Hayward**

Website: **www.wolves.co.uk**

Address: **Molineux Stadium,**

Waterloo Road,

Wolverhampton WV1 4QR

Telephone: **0870 442 0123**

Ticket Office: **01902 687003**

Top Goalscorer 2003-04

Henri Camara - 7 Goals

Final Standings 2003-04

		P	W	D	L	F	A	GD	Pts
18	Leicester	38	3	10	6	19	28	-17	33
19	Leeds	38	5	7	7	25	31	-39	33
20	Wolves	38	7	5	7	23	35	-39	33

All-Time Record - League matches (Home and Away)

Games Played	Won	Drawn	Lost
28	8	8	12

Recent History

Date	Competition	H/A	Result	Scorers
19/04/03	Division 1	A	0-3	
21/12/02	Division 1	H	1-1	Roberts
05/04/02	Division 1	H	1-0	Claridge
31/10/01	Division 1	A	0-1	
02/03/96	Division 1	H	0-1	
26/12/95	Division 1	A	1-1	Malkin
04/12/94	Division 1	H	1-0	Mitchell
22/10/94	Division 1	A	3-3	Cadette, Goodman (2)
20/04/94	Division 1	H	1-0	Mitchell
25/08/93	Division 1	A	0-2	

Player Stats

	Left Foot	Right Foot	Header
Total	2	5	-

% of team's goals: **18%**

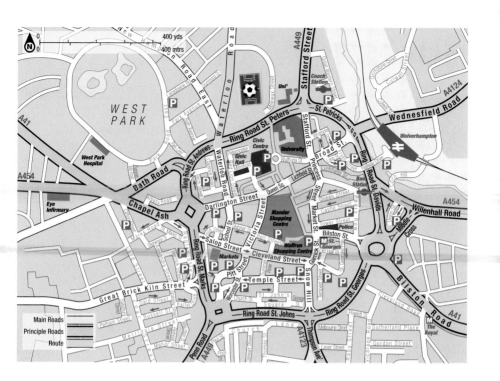

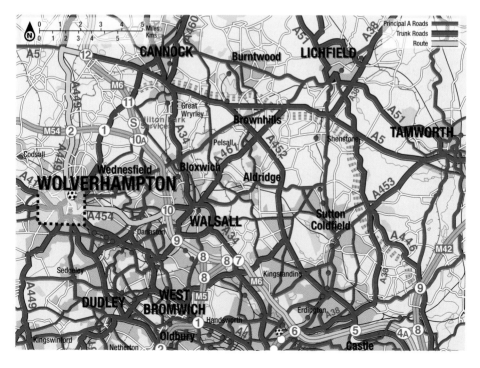

Business Conferences and Meeting

Since its official opening in August 1993, Millwall Conference & Banqueting Centre has become established as a first class venue and host to exhibitions, conferences and product launches.

Our facilities can be tailor-made to match your own specific requirements, from large conferences to small meetings. We can provide a unique environment for your business to conduct a wide range of activities.

We can accommodate almost any event, from a meeting of ten overlooking the football pitch, to over 600 people in our main function suite.

Other benefits include natural daylight and blackout when required; extensive, complimentary on-site parking (except on match days); a well known venue, and surprisingly competitive rates.

The inspirational backdrop of a famous sporting arena generates the perfect atmosphere for your work. We can also offer a behind the scenes tour of the stadium as an addition to your business day.

Millwall Conference & Banqueting Centre is situated at Millwall FC stadium, outside the congestion charging zone, and is only 10 minutes drive from London Bridge and Tower Bridge, with easy access to London City Airport and the new Jubilee Line extension. There is ample on-site parking (not on matchdays).

Our Event Management Team appreciate the importance of your function and will do all we can to ensure that your function is a tremendous success.

For further information or to enquire about booking an event at The Den, please contact: Veronica Quinn, phone: 0207 740 0504, fax: 0207 740 0530

 Millwall Football Club

For further information contact
Matchday Hospitality on 0207 740 0501

Enhanced Fixture List

Date	H/A	Opponent	03-04	Fixture History (last five seasons)	Goals For	Goals Against	Yellow Cards	Red Cards	Biggest Win (season)
Saturday 7 Aug	A	Plymouth Argyle	n/a	Last meeting: 1997-98 Division 2, lost 3-0					
Tuesday 10 Aug	H	Wigan Athletic	2 - 0	DW--W	8	4	6 – 7	0 – 1	3-1 (2000-01)
Saturday 14 Aug	H	Leicester City	n/a	---D-	2	2	3 – 7	0 – 1	-
Saturday 21 Aug	A	Coventry City	0 - 4	--WWL	4	6	7 – 1	0 – 0	3-2 (2002-03)
Saturday 28 Aug	H	Reading	0 - 1	WW-LL	7	3	6 – 8	0 – 0	5-0 (1999-00)
Tuesday 31 Aug	A	Crewe Alexandra	2 - 1	--L-W	2	2	1 – 0	0 – 0	2-1 (2003-04)
Sunday 12 Sep	A	Ipswich Town	3 - 1	---LW	4	5	5 – 2	0 – 0	3-1 (2003-04)
Postposed	H	Derby County	0 - 0	---WD	3	0	2 – 3	0 – 1	3-0 (2002-03)
Saturday 18 Sep	H	Watford	1 - 2	--WWL	6	2	5 – 5	0 – 2	4-0 (2002-03)
Saturday 25 Sep	A	Rotherham United	0 - 0	-LDWD	5	4	5 – 5	0 – 0	3-1 (2002-03)
Postposed	A	Wolves	n/a	--LL-	0	4	2 – 0	0 – 0	-
Saturday 2 Oct	H	Nottingham Forest	1 - 0	--DLW	5	5	7 – 5	1 – 0	1-0 (2003-04)
Saturday 16 Oct	A	Sunderland	1 - 0	----W	1	0	2 – 1	0 – 0	1-0 (2003-04)
Tuesday 19 Oct	H	Gillingham	1 - 2	D-LDL	6	8	2 – 5	0 – 0	-
Saturday 23 Oct	H	Cardiff City	0 - 0	W---D	2	0	2 – 6	1 – 0	2-0 (1999-00)
Saturday 30 Oct	A	Stoke City	0 - 0	LL-WD	4	6	8 – 1	0 – 0	1-0 (2002-03)
Tuesday 2 Nov	A	Queens Park Rangers	n/a	Last meeting: 1989-90 Division 1, drew 0-0					
Friday 5 Nov	H	Sunderland	2 - 1	----W	2	1	0 – 2	0 – 0	2-1 (2003-04)
Saturday 13 Nov	A	Preston North End	2 - 1	L-LLW	5	7	11 – 3	0 – 0	2-1 (2003-04)
Sunday 21 Nov	H	West Ham United	4 - 1	----W	4	1	1 – 1	0 – 1	4-1 (2003-04)
Saturday 27 Nov	A	Burnley	1 - 1	L-DDD	6	7	4 – 3	0 – 0	-
Saturday 4 Dec	H	Sheffield United	2 - 0	--WWW	5	0	7 – 5	2 – 0	2-0 (2003-04)
Saturday 11 Dec	H	Brighton	n/a	---W-	1	0	1 – 2	0 – 1	1-0 (2002-03)
Sunday 19 Dec	A	Leeds United	n/a	Last meeting: 1987-88 Division 2, won 2-1					
Sunday 26 Dec	H	Ipswich Town	0 - 0	---DD	1	1	4 – 2	0 – 1	-
Tuesday 28 Dec	A	Derby County	0 - 2	---WL	2	3	3 – 2	0 – 0	2-1 (2002-03)
Saturday 1 Jan	A	Watford	1 - 3	--WDL	5	4	9 – 9	2 – 1	4-1 (2001-02)
Monday 3 Jan	H	Rotherham United	2 - 1	-WWLW	7	7	5 – 6	0 – 1	4-0 (2000-01)
Saturday 15 Jan	A	Nottingham Forest	2 - 2	--WDD	7	6	5 – 4	1 – 1	2-1 (2001-02)
Saturday 22 Jan	H	Wolves	n/a	--WD-	2	1	6 – 6	0 – 0	1-0 (2001-02)
Saturday 5 Feb	H	Queens Park Rangers	n/a	Last meeting: 1989-90 Division 1, lost 2-1					
Saturday 12 Feb	A	Gillingham	3 - 4	L-LLL	3	8	11 – 6	1 – 0	-
Saturday 19 Feb	H	Stoke City	1 - 1	WW-WD	7	2	8 – 5	0 – 0	3-1 (2002-03)
Tuesday 22 Feb	A	Cardiff City	3 - 1	D---W	4	2	5 – 3	0 – 0	3-1 (2003-04)
Saturday 26 Feb	A	Brighton	n/a	---L-	0	1	2 – 0	0 – 0	-
Saturday 5 Mar	H	Leeds United	n/a	Last meeting: 1987-88 Division 2, won 3-1					
Saturday 12 Mar	A	Wigan Athletic	0 - 0	DL--D	1	2	5 – 2	0 – 0	-
Tuesday 15 Mar	H	Coventry City	2 - 1	--WWW	7	3	3 – 6	1 – 1	2-0 (2002-03)
Saturday 19 Mar	H	Plymouth Argyle	n/a	Last meeting: 1997-98, Division 2, drew 1-1					
Saturday 2 Apr	A	Leicester City	n/a	---L-	1	4	3 – 2	0 – 0	-
Tuesday 5 Apr	A	Reading	0 - 1	LW-LL	4	8	14 – 5	0 – 0	4-3 (2000-01)
Saturday 9 Apr	H	Crewe Alexandra	1 - 1	--W-D	3	1	1 – 5	0 – 0	2-0 (2001-02)
Saturday 16 Apr	A	West Ham United	1 - 1	----D	1	1	2 – 2	0 – 0	-
Saturday 23 Apr	H	Preston North End	0 - 1	L-WWL	4	5	10 – 4	0 – 0	2-1 (2002-03)
Saturday 30 Apr	A	Sheffield United	1 - 2	--LLL	4	8	5 – 4	1 – 0	2-0 (2003-04)
Sunday 8 May	H	Burnley	2 - 0	D-LDW	4	4	4 – 17	1 – 0	2-0 (2003-04)

Football League Championship Fixture Grid 2004-05

(Home ↓ / Away →)	Wolves	Wigan Athletic	West Ham United	Watford	Sunderland	Stoke City	Sheffield United	Rotherham United	Reading	QPR	Preston North End	Plymouth Argyle	Nottingham Forest	Millwall	Leicester City	Leeds United	Ipswich Town	Gillingham	Derby County	Crewe Alexandra	Coventry City	Cardiff City	Burnley	Brighton
Brighton	28/12	21/8	13/11	11/9	30/10	5/3	15/1	30/4	7/8	1/1	5/4	12/3	29/9	11/12	30/8	22/2	27/11	25/9	3/11	16/10	2/4	12/2	16/4	
Burnley	15/3	14/9	28/8	14/8	18/12	3/1	19/3	10/8	2/10	30/10	26/2	4/12	23/4	8/5	18/9	2/11	16/10	9/4	23/2	1/1	7/8	12/3		19/10
Cardiff City	25/9	30/8	5/2	28/12	26/2	5/4	18/12	6/11	13/11	27/11	16/4	2/4	11/9	23/10	19/2	21/8	15/1	11/9	30/4	1/1	10/8		28/9	14/8
Coventry City	20/11	23/10	23/10	9/4	5/3	19/3	11/12	1/1	1/1	19/2	28/9	5/2	23/4	15/3	6/11	11/9	11/9	30/4	4/12	28/8		10/8	19/10	6/11
Crewe Alexandra	18/12	19/10	15/3	15/1	10/8	13/11	19/2	28/9	23/10	28/12	25/9	9/4	5/2	9/4	5/2	30/4	16/4	1/1	30/4		11/9	11/9	27/11	5/2
Derby County	18/12	26/12	22/1	2/10	30/8	16/4	19/2	3/1	21/8	27/11	18/12	12/3	7/8	2/4	13/11	7/8	2/4	13/11		5/4	30/4	18/9	23/10	26/12
Gillingham	2/4	23/4	30/8	8/5	20/11	14/9	4/12	2/10	15/3	3/1	21/8	6/11	18/9	22/1	2/10	8/5	2/4		19/2	18/9	28/9	19/10	26/12	8/5
Ipswich Town	9/4	5/3	18/9	23/10	20/11	14/9	5/2	22/1	19/2	3/1	19/10	28/8	22/1	11/12	26/12	5/3		13/11	10/8	19/3	15/3	2/10	6/11	23/10
Leeds United	14/8	19/2	26/12	22/1	22/1	28/8	27/11	19/10	16/4	2/10	6/11	14/9	16/3	5/3	30/4		13/11	18/12	28/9	11/12	12/2	28/9	2/11	26/2
Leicester City	28/8	20/11	19/2	19/3	15/3	23/4	22/2	28/8	27/11	11/9	16/4	8/5	18/12	14/8		4/12	12/2	28/9	11/9	2/11	16/10	30/10	1/1	26/2
Millwall	tbc	12/3	16/4	1/1	16/10	30/4	25/9	5/4	2/11	13/11	7/8	15/1	2/4		19/12	12/9	12/2	28/12	31/8	21/8	22/2	27/11	22/1	22/1
Nottingham Forest	6/11	7/8	26/12	19/2	14/9	18/9	19/10	5/2	16/4	30/4	23/10	30/8		2/10	5/3	21/8	12/3	27/11	11/12	2/4	6/4	3/1	13/11	11/8
Plymouth Argyle	1/1	6/11	19/2	28/8	15/3	16/4	19/10	5/2	23/10	19/10	28/9		9/4	19/3	23/2	16/10	16/10	30/10	28/12	25/9	3/1	11/12	14/8	30/4
Preston North End	1/1	6/11	19/2	4/12	5/3	19/3	18/9	26/12	15/3	16/4		28/9	14/9	15/1	26/2	23/2	23/4	20/11	11/12	18/9	22/1	11/9	28/8	28/9
QPR	23/10	23/4	6/11	10/8	14/8	2/10	9/4	18/12	12/2		19/10	26/12	18/12	9/4	19/3	18/12	20/11	26/2	3/1	26/12	14/9	28/8	19/2	19/3
Reading	4/12	8/5	10/8	25/9	9/4	16/10	14/8	15/3		5/3	28/8	20/11	2/11	11/12	28/12	2/11	20/11	12/2	1/1	11/9	22/2	23/4	15/1	4/12
Rotherham United	23/4	2/10	14/9	20/11	22/2	2/4	26/2		21/8	7/8	30/8	3/11	13/11	16/4	26/12	8/5	5/4	18/12	30/10	22/1	18/9	16/10	12/3	2/10
Sheffield United	8/5	18/9	3/1	23/4	22/1	12/3		11/12	2/4	30/8	21/8	22/2	12/2	4/12	14/9	5/4	2/11	16/10	20/11	26/2	5/3	7/8	18/12	18/12
Stoke City	19/3	5/2	19/10	4/12	8/5		10/8	14/8	6/11	15/1	11/9	20/11	1/1	19/2	23/10	28/9	28/12	15/3	9/4	23/4	26/2	28/8	25/9	19/2
Sunderland	5/2	5/4	30/4	19/10		27/11	28/9	23/10	30/8	2/4	1/1	1/1	13/11	6/11	15/1	16/4	11/9	19/2	15/1	2/4	7/8	11/12	5/3	3/1
Watford	26/2	22/1	27/11		12/2	30/4	13/11	16/4	26/12	12/3	7/8	30/10	30/8	18/9	21/8	2/11	22/2	2/10	14/9	2/4	23/4	12/3	22/1	23/4
West Ham United	15/1	2/4		8/5	4/12	12/2	11/9	28/12	12/3	11/9	28/12	18/12	12/3	30/8	26/2	1/1	22/2	29/9	21/8	30/8	2/11	5/4	15/3	15/3
Wigan Athletic	11/9		14/8	4/12	28/9	28/8	2/11	1/1	15/1	27/11	13/11	30/4	16/10	16/10	26/2	25/9	12/2	18/12	9/4	28/12	14/9			
Wolves		3/1	2/10	11/12	2/11	7/8	27/11	13/11	30/4	22/2	18/9	12/3	26/12	5/4	16/4	26/12	18/9	19/3						

Millwall Official Yearbook 2004-05
www.millwallfc.co.uk